From Mummies to Microchips
A Case Study in Effective Online Teaching Developed at the University of Manchester

Joyce Tyldesley and Nicky Nielsen

LONDON AND NEW YORK

First published 2020
by Routledge
2 Park Square, Milton Park, Abingdon, Oxon OX14 4RN

and by Routledge
52 Vanderbilt Avenue, New York, NY 10017

Routledge is an imprint of the Taylor & Francis Group, an informa business

© 2020 Joyce Tyldesley and Nicky Nielsen

The right of Joyce Tyldesley and Nicky Nielsen to be identified as authors of this work has been asserted by them in accordance with sections 77 and 78 of the Copyright, Designs and Patents Act 1988.

All rights reserved. No part of this book may be reprinted or reproduced or utilised in any form or by any electronic, mechanical, or other means, now known or hereafter invented, including photocopying and recording, or in any information storage or retrieval system, without permission in writing from the publishers.

Trademark notice: Product or corporate names may be trademarks or registered trademarks, and are used only for identification and explanation without intent to infringe.

British Library Cataloguing-in-Publication Data
A catalogue record for this book is available from the British Library

Library of Congress Cataloging-in-Publication Data
A catalog record for this book has been requested

ISBN: 978-0-367-40627-1 (hbk)
ISBN: 978-0-367-80938-6 (ebk)

Typeset in Times New Roman
by Apex CoVantage, LLC

From Mummies to Microchips

This volume offers a detailed case study of the internationally acclaimed online programmes in Egyptology at the University of Manchester, UK. It distils over a decade of online teaching experience and student feedback, providing guidance for instructors developing their own online offerings.

Today, many universities are actively encouraging their teaching staff towards the development of:

- online programmes (programmes to be taught entirely online) and/or
- online units (units to be incorporated into "blended" programmes taught partially online and partially face-to-face).

Unfortunately, the staff tasked with the development of online learning rarely have access to the expertise that they need to help them utilise their teaching skills to their full potential. Technical assistance may be provided by the university e-learning department, but pedagogical and practical help – the support of colleagues with many years' experience teaching online – is lacking.

Written by experts, the book provides an invaluable guide for those wishing – or being compelled – to establish their own online courses within the humanities.

Joyce Tyldesley is Reader in Egyptology at the University of Manchester, where she teaches a suite of online courses including the world's first online MA in Egyptology. She wrote the highly successful MOOC "Ancient Egypt: A History in Six Objects". Joyce studied the archaeology of the Eastern Mediterranean at Liverpool University, then obtained a D.Phil. in prehistoric archaeology from Oxford University. She holds an honorary doctorate from the University of Bolton. She is a research associate of the Manchester Museum and a senior fellow of the Higher Education Academy. Joyce has published more than 20 books and many articles, including three television tie-in books and *Cleopatra, Last Queen of Egypt*, which was a Radio 4 "Book of the Week". She has published three books for children, and her play for children, *The Lost Scroll*, premiered at Kendal Museum in April 2011. *Tutankhamen's Curse: The Developing History of an Egyptian King* (US title *Tutankhamen*) won the Felicia A. Holton Book Award from the Archaeological Institute of America. Her most recent book is *Nefertiti's Face: The Creation of an Icon*.

Nicky Nielsen is Lecturer in Online Egyptology at the University of Manchester, teaching on the Certificate, Diploma, Short Courses and MA Egyptology programmes. Originally from Denmark, Nicky was awarded an AHRC Block Grant to undertake PhD research at the University of Liverpool investigating subsistence strategies and craft production at the Ramesside fortress site of Zawiyet Umm el-Rakham. He has excavated in Europe, Turkey and Egypt and is currently field director of the University of Liverpool Tell Nabasha Survey Project. He is a fellow of the Higher Education Academy. Alongside a series of scholarly papers, Nicky has recently published *Pharaoh Seti I: Father of Egyptian Greatness*.

Contents

List of figures	vii
Acknowledgements	viii

	Introduction: kingpin of the educational situation JOYCE TYLDESLEY	1
1	Distance education: the past, the present and the future NICKY NIELSEN	6
2	Beneath the bandages: teaching Egyptology Online JOYCE TYLDESLEY	21
3	Activities: sparking student engagement JOYCE TYLDESLEY	46
4	Assessment strategies: problems and solutions JOYCE TYLDESLEY	60
5	Lectures and podcasts: creation and optimal use NICKY NIELSEN	66
6	Informal online resources and MOOCs NICKY NIELSEN	77
7	Mumford the Mummy: online Egyptology for children JOYCE TYLDESLEY	82

Conclusion: helpful hints for setting up an online course 86
JOYCE TYLDESLEY

Index 90

Figures

2.1	Certificate Programme Icons	30
2.2	Short Courses: Screenshot showing weekly learning modules for Queens of Ancient Egypt. The discussion boards are accessed via the left-hand menu.	33
2.3	The Diploma Programme Home Page: Site of the units and learning modules	35
2.4	A Linked System of Online Programmes and Learning Experiences	36
2.5	Changing learning environments across the credit-bearing programmes	37
3.1	A selection of MA discussion boards, showing closed and open boards	48
5.1	Schematic Overview: The development of lecturing technologies utilised on the Manchester Egyptology Online programmes from 2004 to the current day	70
7.1	Mumford on Screen	83
7.2	Mumford the Mummy	84

Acknowledgements

Many colleagues and friends have contributed to the evolution of Egyptology Online and the "Manchester Method" of online Egyptology. We would particularly like to acknowledge the help and support given by Kate Hilton and Ian Miller of the Faculty of Life Sciences eLearning team, our tireless course administrators Anne Pinkerton and Lisa Monks, and Dr Glenn Godenho of Liverpool University, who spent many years working on our developing suite of online programmes and learning experiences. Finally, we would like to express our gratitude for the support and feedback given year after year by our students. Thanks everyone: we could not have done this without you.

Joyce Tyldesley and Nicky Nielsen

Introduction
Kingpin of the educational situation
Joyce Tyldesley

Picture the scene. A meeting in the Department of Archaeology, or Art History, or any other university-taught humanities subject in Britain. The room smells of stale coffee and of the cheese and pickle sandwiches unwisely provided as lunch (for this is a lunchtime meeting – the working lunch being an almost daily necessity in a busy department running scores of timetabled classes). The assembled lecturers are being told that their traditional teaching methods are now outdated. They must, with immediate effect, start to include an element of online learning in their programmes. Of course, funding is tight or non-existent in this small department, so this is something that staff will be expected to implement in their own time. Technical support may be available from the already overworked IT support team, but there is no one to offer practical advice on course design or content because, although there has been a lot of recent talk about online learning at high levels within the faculty, it has all been theoretical. No one has actually done it. Those in authority are convinced, however, that this lack of experience is not a problem. How difficult can it be, to put tried and tested course material online? There can be no looking back! The staff are to go away and come back in a week's time with a plan that will move the suddenly out-of-date department forward into the modern world, saving a great deal of money in the process.

This scene may seem exaggerated, but as many academics will testify, it is not so very far from the truth. Rapid advances in digital technology have moved distance and flexible learning from a niche speciality to a basic educational tool, and British universities have slowly but surely started to wake up to the potential of the virtual classroom and less formal online learning. After many years during which the Open University, the UK's flagship provider of flexible and part-time teaching, was regrettably all too often regarded as a lesser educational establishment, the provision of conspicuous online courses is suddenly seen as a sign that a university has assumed its rightful place alongside other global educators.[1]

The benefits of online learning are obvious. By using the virtual classroom, universities are able to connect with high-achieving students worldwide, students who otherwise could never dream of attending a traditional, face-to-face programme at a campus university.[2] For these students, learning while earning or while otherwise tied to the home is suddenly a real possibility. While older students – those returning to education after a lifetime in the workplace – might feel somewhat daunted by this brave new educational world, younger students – those who cannot remember life without a tablet or smart phone, and who have been using iPads since their nursery days – simply see it as a logical use of available technologies.

Increasing online student numbers bring an obvious financial reward to the university, as the extra students bring with them extra tuition fees. Even when the approach is to adopt blended learning – to introduce an e-learning element into an pre-existing, face-to-face course with no expectation of raised student numbers – there will be savings in costs (lower heating, lighting, equipment, paper, building maintenance etc.), while the new flexibility makes timetabling so much easier for both administrators and students. It is little wonder that in 2018 an estimated 270,000 UK undergraduate students and 108,000 postgraduate students were studying for their degrees wholly or partially online.[3] To these can be added those who are taking advantage of the less formal and non-credit-bearing courses offered by many universities. Egyptology Online at the University of Manchester, a small centre with just two permanent staff-members, has been able to reach 20,000 plus students in a year, using a combination of MOOCs, short credit-bearing courses and formally credited programmes. In any given week, there are likely to be upwards of 5,000 students engaged with one of our offerings.

It seems that everyone is a winner. But what of the lecturer, suddenly charged with creating appropriate online content? In the words of philosopher and educationalist Sidney Hook (1946: 172),

> All plans for educational reforms depend on the teacher for their proper realization. Unless carried out by personnel sincerely imbued with the philosophy animating the reforms and trained in the arts of effective teaching, they are doomed to failure. Everyone who remembers his own educational experience remembers teachers, not methods and techniques. The teacher is the kingpin of the educational situation, He makes and breaks programs.

The newly appointed "kingpin" is likely to be bursting with questions:

- Should face-to-face material simply be put unthinkingly online, or should there be a change in presentation to meet the different demands

and expectation of online learners as outlined, for example, by Bonk (2007)?
- Where does he or she start to build a course that both engages students and promotes learning, providing a parallel experience to face-to-face teaching?
- How does he or she adjust the traditional teacher's role to allow students to work online to their full potential?

Some UK universities have developed strategies to deal with this. They may treat their online programmes as entirely separate to their campus offerings[4] or may have developed a tight university-wide distance-learning strategy.[5] However, these large mechanisms are not available to all and are in any case irrelevant to the lecturer who is simply wanting to introduce the element of online content that will convert a face-to-face course into a blended learning course. With little or no advice available, the lecturer could be forgiven for falling into a state of mild panic.

At the University of Manchester, Egyptology (the study of the culture and language of ancient Egypt) has been taught entirely online for over a decade. This approach fascinates many non-Egyptophiles, who tend to see Egyptology as either a dull, library-based hobby pursued by elderly academics or as an action-packed physical "fortune and glory" type adventure. Nothing could be further from the truth. Having evolved as recently as 1822 with the decoding of the hieroglyphic script, Egyptology is a fast moving, multi-disciplinary subject that makes great use of the opportunities offered by the internet. Museums have developed websites that open their collections up to the widest possible audience; excavations have created websites that allow unprecedented access to archaeological discoveries; newsgroups, blogs and tweets all allow the rapid dissemination and discussion of ideas. The computer, rather than the trowel, is the essential tool of the modern Indiana Jones.

In 2007 I was appointed to oversee the development of the university's fledgling online Certificate in Egyptology programme. Today I oversee a suite of online courses ranging from a MOOC to the world's first online master's in Egyptology programme. This has not been an easy journey, but it has been a rewarding and informative one. Working first with Dr Glenn Godenho and more recently with my co-author, Dr Nicky Nielsen, I have had the opportunity to observe, develop and refine online teaching methods over a decade of experimentation, implementation and peer and student feedback. This experience forms the core of this book.

From Mummies to Microchips is a case study in online teaching in the UK. It is a practical guide rather than a theoretical study, so references to pedagogic literature have been kept to a minimum. This longitudinal approach offers the reader a history of problems encountered and the solutions devised to overcome them. Starting with the necessary background to the case study, Chapter 1 provides an exploration of the history of distance and online learning, while Chapter 2 contributes a history of online Egyptology within the University of Manchester. Chapters 3–5 then explore three specific, problematic aspects of online teaching and learning:

- How do we encourage off-campus students to engage with the programme content, with the staff and with each other?
- How do we assess work submitted online?
- How do we present the online lecture effectively?

Finally, Chapters 6 and 7 look beyond the traditional university environment to consider the use of online material as both outreach and a recruiting tool. Readers too stressed, too eager or too time-poor to read the entire book might like to start by reading the Conclusion, which lists 22 helpful hints for those engaged in setting up an online course.

From Mummies to Microchips does not offer a one-stop solution to all the difficulties encountered in online learning: that would be impossible. Every discipline brings its own quirks and foibles, and there can be no one-size-fits-all format to online teaching, just as there can be no one-size-fits-all format to face-to-face teaching. But, written in an accessible and (I like to think) friendly style and resting on a sound pedagogical base, it does provide an honest and practical account of the development of a successful suite of online courses. In so doing it offers solutions to frequently encountered problems that will be familiar to teachers in all disciplines. Alongside this, it offers references to relevant pedagogical publications that the reader new to online teaching will find useful. It is the book that I wish I could have read before starting my career as an online teacher. I hope that you find it useful.

Notes

1. The history of the Open University is documented in the Open University Digital Archive (OUDA); a selection of this material is available to view online: www.open.ac.uk/library/digital-archive/
2. Of course, only relatively wealthy students are able to participate in online learning, an obvious fact that is nevertheless frequently overlooked. The often-heard assumption that "everyone has a smart phone" is far from true.
3. Complete University Guide 2019: www.thecompleteuniversityguide.co.uk/distance-learning/what-is-distance-learning/
4. Liverpool University, for example, promotes itself as "pursuing excellence in online learning since 2001", having developed a successful partnership with Laureate Online Education. The university retains control of the curricula, staff members and assessment of students.

5 University of Manchester Worldwide (UMW) was created in 2017 to develop online courses that would allow students the flexibility to study anytime, anywhere, while supporting academic staff who are developing teaching methods and materials designed for the digital age. However, not all University of Manchester online teaching goes through UMW. This book does not discuss the programmes and teaching philosophy of UMW.

Works cited

Bonk, C. J. (2007). *The World Is Open: How Web Technology Is Revolutionising Education.* San Francisco: Jossey-Bass.

Hook, S. (1946). *Education for Modern Man.* New York: Dial Press.

1 Distance education
The past, the present and the future
Nicky Nielsen

The aim of this chapter is to investigate the development of distance education from its origins as humble correspondence courses focusing on the teaching of short hand writing in the early 18th century to the current globe-spanning industry of e-learning courses, programmes and degrees. The chapter will also consider the future opportunities and threats against distance learning and discuss the various scholarly arguments regarding the broader usefulness of distance education in terms of providing high-value content, student retention, student experience and its comparison to face-to-face courses.

The past

The origin of distance education can be dated with some certainty to 1728. In the March edition of the *Boston Gazette* the teacher Caleb Philipps advertised a course on the newly developed shorthand method of writing ("As this way of Joyning (*sic*) 3, 4, 5 &c words in one in every Sentence by the Moods, Tenses, Persons, and Verb; do's not in the least spoil the Long Hand" (n.a. 1728), Philipps assured his potential students). As an addendum to the advertisement Philipps noted that: "Any Persons in the Country desirous to Learn this Art, may be having several Lessons sent Weekly to them, be as perfectly Instructed as those that live in Boston."

Philipps' assurance that those who learnt at a distance would receive the same quality of education as those learning with him at his town house in King's Street is a principle which, as Chapter 5 will highlight, remains a subject of intense debate and scrutiny. Philipps' decision to market his teaching with a distance learning component was revolutionary in its way, although it was most likely born of a simple desire to attract a larger potential customer base as well as an awareness of the various issues surrounding even short-distance travels in the 18th century. A similar early attempt at establishing distance education can be found more than a century later in an advertisement in the Swedish newspaper *Lunds Weckoblad* from 1833, which offered both men and women the opportunity to study literary composition through "the medium of the post" (quoted by Holmberg 1995).[1]

The concept of distance education was further developed and formalised in the mid-19th century by the educator Sir Isaac Pitman (1813–97). The introduction of standardised postage rates across England in 1840 allowed Pitman to teach shorthand writing to students all over the country by sending and receiving lessons on postcards which he then marked and returned, along with relevant feedback. Pitman's idea quickly broadened into more diverse correspondence courses, in particular through the efforts of the German language teacher Gustav Langenscheidt (1832–95), who, together with his colleague Charles Toussaint, developed a method for self-learning the French language (*Unterrichtsbriefe zur Erlernung der Französischen Sprache*), which he published in 1856 (Bower and Hardy 2004). Other educational establishments such as Ruskin College and the University of London soon followed suit and by the late 19th century had established their own correspondence courses (Kulich 1970).

In the United States the development of distance education was initially fuelled by the author and educational pioneer Anna Eliot Ticknor (1823–96), who in 1873 founded the Society to Encourage Studies at Home, an organisation where female tutors taught female students via exchanges of letters (Bergmann 2001) but also facilitated access to teaching materials by establishing a large lending collection numbering several thousand volumes. Student retention and progress was assessed through frequent examinations, and most of the teaching consisted of recommended readings and personal correspondence with tutors (Bower and Hardy 2004). The range of topics taught was mainly focused in the humanities, with the focus being on English, history, science, French, German and art. Despite a lack of public awareness of the course and marketing, the Society to Encourage Studies at Home enrolled and taught more than 7,000 women during its roughly 20-year existence (Caruth and Caruth 2013).

The Illinois Wesleyan University followed suit the year afterwards and opened a correspondence course which led to a bachelor degree. Plans were afoot to expand the provision to a master's programme and even a doctorate, but in 1910, the correspondence course was closed despite its popular appeal as other institutions refused to accept degrees granted on the basis of distance learning (Kulich 1970).

However, even despite this somewhat unwarranted resistance, correspondence courses became further ingrained into educational establishments. In 1881 the Baptist cleric and linguist William Rainey Harper (1856–1906) of the Chautauqua School of Languages launched – at the request of students in his Hebrew class – a correspondence course teaching ancient and modern languages. When Harper was promoted to the role of president at the University of Chicago, he took his experience in distance education and correspondence courses with him and continued broadening the use of distance education within the formal university environment (Harting and Erthal 2005). Following the success of such courses at Chicago, other institutions – notably the University of Wisconsin and the University of West Virginia – instituted similar courses (Holmberg, 2005).

Simultaneously with this development in the United States, pioneering institutions focusing on distance education also began to appear in the United Kingdom, such as Skerry's College in Edinburgh, founded in 1878 and focusing on preparing candidates for entry exams to the Civil Service and university entry exams via correspondence courses. Other institutions dedicated to correspondence courses also included the Foulks Lynch Correspondence Tuition Service, founded in 1884, the University Correspondence College in Cambridge, founded in 1887, and the Diploma Correspondence College in Oxford, founded in 1894 (Holmberg, 2005).

A further milestone in the development of distance learning occurred in 1909 when the Australian state of Victoria began offering distance education programmes taught at secondary level (Stacey and Visser 2005). Australia, as the sixth-largest country on earth and with a widely distributed small population of around 5 million, was faced with unique challenges and possibilities in the incorporation of distance learning into every level of its educational system. In 1911, the University of Queensland followed suit by offering degree programmes obtained through distance learning (Holmberg, 2005), and in 1914 the State of Victoria expanded its provision of distance learning to include secondary education, soon followed by other states (Stacey and Visser 2005). The success of the Australian programme was such that in 1931, Kenneth Cunningham, the inaugural director of the Australian Council for Educational Research, stated that:

> Australia can claim to be the first country to have shown in a systematic way, and on a large scale, that it was possible to provide by correspondence education a complete primary and secondary education for children who had never been to school.
>
> (Cunningham 1931: 9)

But distance education did not only benefit those in formal schooling or higher education. Following a series of tragic accidents and death related to mining in Pennsylvania in the 1880s, the Pennsylvania state legislature passed the Mine Safety Act of 1885, intending to ensure better working conditions for miners and fewer industrial accidents. However, the law required all miners to take a written safety examination, a stipulation which had the unintended side effect of placing many of the uneducated miners in danger of losing their jobs (Watkinson 1996). The newspaper editor and publisher Thomas J. Foster (Gaumnitz 1952) used his newspaper, *The Mining Herald* in Shenandoah, Pennsylvania, to help alleviate the issue by printing sample problems from the test and inviting miners to send questions and comments to be printed in the newspaper. He further developed this initial concept to a series of correspondence courses aimed at helping miners to achieve promotions to mine supervisors and foremen. This eventually led to the foundation of the International Correspondence School in Scranton, Pennsylvania, which by the end of the 19th century was offering courses not just within the United States but also to students as far afield as Australia and Mexico (Bower and Hardy 2004).

The spread of correspondence education continued during the first half of the 20th century. To many, the system provided an opportunity not just to obtain degrees and classifications but to improve their changes of promotion, better jobs and a higher quality of life. People with little formal education were afforded a more flexible second chance at education, a flexibility which appealed to many in full-time work or who had duties of care.

The Hermod Institute in Sweden provides an excellent case study for this development. Founded in 1889 as the *Malmö Språk- och Handelsinstitut* (Malmö Language and Mercantile Institute) by Hans Svensson Hermod, the school began offering correspondence courses in 1898. In 1906 the range of programmes were extended to cover foreign languages such as English, and in 1911 the institute incorporated a range of disciplines, including law and agriculture. By the 1930s the institute had more than 50,000 students worldwide per year. Hermods still remains in existence, catering to roughly 60,000 students per year via distance learning, focusing on education and coaching through high schools, polytechnics and adult education (Gaddén 1973).

As technology continued to develop and evolve from the early 20th century onwards, so did correspondence and distance education. The spread of the radio following the First World War prompted radio stations to offer distance learning courses via broadcasts or audio recordings (Bower and Hardy 2004). With the development of television during the 1920s and 1930s, other educational pioneers such as J.C. Stobart and R.C.G. Williams promoted "televised universities" – essentially lectures broadcast via the BBC (Katana, Katans and Vavere 2012).

Through the 1940s and 1950s, audio recordings, video recordings and broadcasts continued to complement the mail-based correspondence courses. The mass appeal and broad reach of distance education also interested politicians of various leanings, and in 1969 the UK Labour Government under Harold Wilson took the step of founding an institution dedicated to widening access to the highest standards of scholarship: the Open University (Dorey 2015).

Apart from mail correspondence, the Open University also utilised scheduled BBC broadcasts as part of their educational arsenal, along with video and audio recordings. More importantly, the Open University offered a structured framework for learning, but also assessment, quality assurance and the conferring of degrees (issues surrounding the right and relevant charters to confer degrees crops up frequently when studying some of the pioneering institutions offering distance education). The methods and foundational principles of the Open University were soon copied throughout the world, and variants appeared in the United States, Latin America and all over Europe.

The interest of the state in the spread of distance learning represented a definitive break from most governments' attitude to distance learning – one of dismissal, suspicion and outright derision. With the foundation of the Open University and similar institutions: "The image of distance education changed almost all over the world from one of possibly estimable but little respected or even pathetic endeavour to one of a publicly acknowledged promise of innovation" (Holmberg, 2005: 21).

The development and spread of the World Wide Web during the 1980s and 1990s represent perhaps the largest opportunity and also general upheaval in the history of distance education. The internet represents all incarnations of previous learning methods: writing, audio and visual learning tools can be employed and merged in ways that early pioneers such as Pitman and Ticknor could only have dreamed off. With the increased pace of technological development, new tools appear on a weekly basis, making it near impossible for any course tutor or director to keep up.

Writing at the very cusp of this development, Taylor made the point that distance learning educators were more inclined to embrace new technologies in an effort to overcome what he dubbed the "Tyranny of Isolation" – the widely acknowledged tendency for distance learning students to feel detached from their programme, fellow students and course tutors:

> While distance educators have striven to overcome the perceived limitations associated with limited opportunities for face to face teaching arising from the "tyranny of distance", on-campus educators appear to be basically satisfied with conventional approaches and therefore have tended to ignore the new technologies of teaching and to concentrate their energies on research and other forms of scholarly activities.
> (Taylor 1995: 1)

Taylor's paper proposes four stages or generations of distance learning through history: (1) the Correspondence Model, utilising mainly written materials; (2) the Multi-Media Model, which, alongside written materials utilises audio recordings, video recordings, broadcasts and computer based learning materials; (3) the Telelearning Model, utilising information technologies to heighten communication within the cohort and between the tutor and the cohort by using tele- and videoconferencing tools and other communication systems; and (4) the Flexible Learning Model, which Taylor envisaged as incorporating "the benefits of high quality CD-ROM based interactive multimedia (IMM), with the enhanced interactivity and access to an increasingly extensive range of teaching-learning resources offered by connection to the Internet" (Taylor 1995: 1–2).

The CD-ROM has, since Taylor's paper, largely gone the way of the dodo, but there is a deeper truth in his description of the Flexible Learning Model. The spread of the internet does allow both for the sharing of higher quality materials in the form of lectures, PowerPoints, PDFs, and interactive videos and 3D models, for instance; it also allows for faster and higher quality communication. While those of us who teach widely spaced international cohorts still face certain daunting challenges relating to – for instance – the live-streaming of lectures (a difficult feat when a cohort can include students based in Australia, Germany and Costa Rica), developing technologies nevertheless allow for new tools for potentially overcoming such obstacles to the satisfaction of both educators and students.

In his seminal work on the development of distance education Holmberg identified two major characteristics of 21st-century online distance education (also called e-learning): the possibility of asynchronous communication between students and tutor in the form of message boards leading to a greater degree of flexibility, as students do not need to adhere to a predetermined timetable, and the sheer availability of material on the World Wide Web, leading, to "practically unlimited quantities of information" available at the click of a button (Holmberg, 2005: 27–8).

The apparent ease with which information can be made available unsurprisingly led to a number of poor quality courses being offered and a range of bad practices – some evidently exploitative and focusing wholly on profit rather than providing useful and educational content – which helped to initially give e-learning a bad reputation in scholarly circles (Holmberg, 2005), even leading some scholars to prophesise that e-learning would eventually bring about the downfall of higher education altogether.

However, despite its varied history of success and failure, the development of distance education represents at heart a very human desire to learn and to better our condition and lot in life. From the students who answered Caleb Philipps' advertisement in the *Boston Gazette* wishing to learn the new and exciting writing style of shorthand, to the 21st-century student who signs up for an online MBA, there is a shared drive towards learning, one which distance education in a variety of forms, and with a range of tools, has helped to realise over the course of nearly three centuries.

The present

Distance learning, in particular online distance learning, is a teaching method in constant flux and development, buffeted by rapidly developing technologies and equally rapidly developing pedagogical theories and methodologies. Today, the foundational literature on online distance learning may appear at once prescient and outdated. Speculations by authors such as Rowntree (1995) – who pointed out a number of potential pitfalls to online distance learning, including technological problems: "I don't pretend to understand the intricacies of networked computer systems, communications soft-ware, inadequate bandwidths and recalcitrant modems. But I do know they can cause problems, especially for students trying to join the course from certain countries abroad" (Rowntree 1995: 212) – along with some very succinct and still poignant comments about both the risk of student alienation and tutor overload (1995: 214) have to some extent been born out. Other early speculations such as that of Harry (1992: 190), who felt that developing telecommunication technologies would most likely be employed for university administration but not necessarily for teaching, have not.

Other foundational literature on the topic of e-learning in particular raised issues surrounding the degree to which various subtle visual cues – communicated largely subconsciously in the classroom – could effectively be translated to an online medium. In 2001, Neal argued that: "Currently, neither synchronous nor asynchronous distance-learning technologies capture the wealth of visual cues and expressiveness found in face-to-face classroom experiences." Neal took particular issue with the performative aspects of lecturing, termed "storytelling". In synchronous recorded lectures, she observed a tendency for instructors to sanitise their lectures, leaving out humorous asides and similar digressions. Among the solutions proposed by Neal to address the issue of stilted delivery was utilising a combination of synchronous and asynchronous techniques – in other words to record a lecture in front of a live audience and make it available to an asynchronous audience, very much like modern-day lecture capture technology. The extent to which this method would have worked is debatable even to this day: a 2019 survey of higher education lecturers using (or being compelled to use) lecture capture to record live lectures showed that a large portion of participants (50.8%) still felt that having lectures recorded hindered their spontaneity.

Despite multiple teething troubles, distance learning using the medium of the internet has become a staple of both higher education and vocational courses as well as management and staff training. Determining a precise number of students who study online is complicated by the definition of what constitutes online study. As e-learning has grown in prominence it has given rise not just to "pure" online programmes and courses but also to blended learning courses where some teaching materials are made available online. Beyond that, the vast majority of courses – at least in UK higher education – have dedicated online spaces such as Blackboard where course information, assessment dropboxes, lecture PDFs and even discussion groups can be uploaded and maintained. As such, it is essentially inconceivable that any UK undergraduate student would make it through three years of university without receiving – in some shape or form – at least part of their teaching through an online medium.

With the proliferation of lecture capture across universities in the UK and elsewhere, this tendency has of course only increased. But if students who study online are defined as students who take at least one unit or module wholly online during their programme, then the percentage of students who study online, at least in the United States, stands at around one-third. Out of this cohort, 15.4% studied exclusively online in 2018 (Lederman 2018). In the United Kingdom, in 2016–17, 8% of students studied wholly online, a large majority of them through the Open University, with those based in other institutions making up only 35% (*Flexible Learning: The Current State of Play 2018*). Despite these high (and growing) numbers, distance learning in many UK universities still appears somewhat of an "add-on", driven largely by financial incentives combined with a desire on the part of management to highlight their institution's cutting-edge learning technologies rather than by any deeper understanding of what special requirements and compromises distance learning actually requires.

This lack of understanding perhaps also explains the abnormally high drop-out rates that continue to plague distance learning courses, currently standing between 40% and 80% on average. While differences between student expectation and reality may in part explain the high drop-out rate, this is surely also the case with face-to-face courses, which do not have such high drop-out rates. In reality, distance learning students – in particular those who study wholly online – are less physically shackled to a specific programme or university. They have not – mostly – moved to a new city, they have not moved jobs or even physically relocated to a new country to study. They do not live in university accommodation which they would have to vacate if they left the course. Distance learners lack these physical anchors, and that makes dropping out a simpler process, often requiring little more than a few emails. To this perhaps can be added a sense, sometimes found both in management, administration and in faculty lounges, that distance learning should somehow play second fiddle to face-to-face teaching and that – by extension – distance learners are second-class students. When this attitude is born out and noticed by the distance learners themselves, it is hardly surprising that they chose to leave their programmes.

A simple example of this attitude from a UK university is the rights of distance learning students to be issued student cards. Distance learners will of course not need these to get in and out of buildings on campus, but museums and shops all over the world provide discounts and sometimes free entry to holders of such cards and – given that the online cohort in question were charged the same fee as traditional students, it was of course felt by the teaching staff that they should be given the same perks. The university in question did not act on this advice, and some distance learners did not receive their student cards until months later and only after extensive wrangling and discussion within the university about whether distance learners really had the "right" to such cards. Such an attitude is pure poison to any distance learning course, because when the distance learning students find out, they will quite understandably be asking themselves whether their university really values them at all or whether they would be better off taking their custom elsewhere. And "custom" is the key word. As higher education for better or (more probably) for worse becomes increasingly marketised, so does distance learning. Online students still have more limited choice than traditional students, with fewer distance learning courses in particular subjects available worldwide. But this state of affairs will not continue. As e-learning becomes more prevalent, so will the choices for distance learners expand. And if institutions persist in treating distance learners as a convenient afterthought, they will simply be able to go elsewhere at the push of a button.

The issue of student retention in online and distance learning has been a frequently discussed issue since the start of the millennium (see for instance Simpson 2003, 2004, as well as Heyman 2010). In a recent contribution to the ongoing debate of how to effectively retain students in an online learning environment, Pierrakeas et al. (2019) utilised data from the Hellenic Open University to provide an overview of the main reasons why distance learning students dropped out of programmes. Among those most frequently cited were obligations by adult learners, who constitute by far the largest section of students studying wholly online, as well as miscalculations on the part of the student of the amount of time and effort required in online study. The authors argued that by using learning algorithms to automatically predict and identify students at risk of dropping out from their behaviour, drop-out rates could be lowered. While this method is interesting and carries a great degree of potential, it also appears experimental for now and so is unlikely to be effectively replicated at multiple institutions – at least in the near future. The study does however underline an important handicap facing distance learning tutors. Given the geographical distance between tutor and student, it is perhaps sometimes too easy for a single struggling student to become essentially invisible. It remains therefore crucial that frequent communication between tutor and student takes place. For the Egyptology courses at the University of Manchester, this communication takes the form of weekly discussion boards where students are required to post written replies or solutions to seminar questions, quizzes or other informal assessments. As well as teaching the students – in combination with pre-recorded lectures, podcasts, vlogs and documentary style videos, as well as written material – the boards allow tutors to effectively monitor student participation and frequently allow tutors to identify students who are struggling and have either stopped posting or whose posting frequency has notably changed.

While some factors behind student drop-out rates – notably changes in life circumstances, changing responsibilities in particular for adult learners and of course financial issues – are difficult to directly influence or mitigate from a tutor perspective, others such as low student engagement leading to disillusionment with the course are not. Increasing student engagement has a clear and direct influence on student retention in traditional face-to-face courses and there is little reason to think it does not have a similar effect on distance learning courses. In order to improve student engagement on a distance learning course, educators can for instance employ a variant of the flipped-classroom approach (as argued by Keene 2013; McLaughlin et al. 2013) or try alternatively integrating alternative teaching methods such as student-to-student mentoring as part of the curriculum design (see for instance Boyle et al. 2010).

Ideally, a combination of such strategies should be employed rather than relying upon a single strategy. Like traditional teaching, distance learning requires above all a flexible teaching strategy, a methodology that both takes into account the need for distance learners to be treated like "regular" students – and certainly under no circumstances to be discriminated against because of the online nature of their courses – but also an awareness that distance learners face a unique set of challenges less common to traditional students, challenges that manifest in lower student retention rates for online courses. The implementation of innovative pedagogical strategies can mitigate to some extent such challenges. But pedagogical innovation is not enough. An awareness of developing technologies that can further bolster student retention and, more broadly, help to further develop distance learning is also crucial, as is an awareness of both political and economic factors which may influence the future development and direction of distance learning.

The future

In early 2019 the market value of educational software reached an astonishing 5.37 billion USD. This translates to thousands of individual types of software developed and marketed on an annual basis catering to students and learners at every level. In such as fast-moving and hectic field it is imperative that the choice to select new software and trial new technologies is not exclusively the responsibility (or indeed preserve) of the programme or unit coordinators and teaching staff, but that the institutions set up well-funded and comprehensive e-learning teams (rather than, for instance, place the responsibility for distance learning on the shoulders of already-overworked IT departments). A cooperative and symbiotic relationship between the academic teaching staff and the technical expertise found in a dedicated e-learning team is crucial to the continued spread and success of e-learning within higher education. Some universities have experimented with setting up separate departments dedicated exclusively to distance learning, a virtual campus of a sort, catering to students throughout the world. This is no doubt an effective way forward if, of course, it does not fall foul to the prevalent institutional desire to standardise uncritically. Not all courses are the same and not all distance learning strategies can be employed on all programmes and units. There is a world of difference between teaching a group of 200 MBA students all based in the same remote campus in, for instance, Dubai or Hong Kong and teaching 12 students from 12 different countries Classical philosophy. Flexibility and a genuine respect for the student cohort as a real and genuine part of the university – not simply a way to make a few quick bucks – is crucial in the success of any distance learning endeavour.

Perhaps the most hotly anticipated and also revolutionary addition to the cadre of distance learning tools will be the cost-effective implementation of 360° virtual photo or video tours, virtual reality (VR) and augmented reality (AR). Virtual reality is by no means a new addition to distance learning. VR was utilised to provide training and educational content from at least the mid-1990s onwards (see for instance Moore 1995; Rickel and Johnson 1998), and virtual reality flight simulators have been used in some form since the first half of the 20th century. However, in the last decade the development of virtual reality has exploded both as a result of the increased power of computers in private ownership, allowing developers to market higher quality products, but also as a result of the spread of smartphones with high definition displays. The latter have allowed cheap, mass-produced headsets such as Google Cardboard which simply require the customer to insert their smartphone and then play an interactive video or other 3D environment directly through the medium of their phone. The development of the Oculus Rift, its sale to Facebook for the sum of 2 billion USD and its subsequent public release in 2016 no doubt helped push further developments in the

Distance education 17

field. And with each development, each new public model, the price of good VR headsets and software drops. Already now universities and other institutions are not just experimenting with this new technology for the purposes of creating new teaching methodologies, they are actively rolling them out both in online and traditional classroom settings. For an Egyptologist the prospect is fascinating. It is impossible to bring a class of 50 students on a day trip to the Valley of the Kings, which means that traditional lecture tools have to be employed – slides, images, videos. But with the relatively small cost of a classroom's supply of Google Cardboard or similar low-cost headsets and access to either publicly available or specially created 360° virtual photo or video tours, students can be taken on virtual fieldtrips into tombs, into temples, through the desert, wherever a camera and a cameraperson can conceivably go. The University of Melbourne already employs a 3D VR model of the Tomb of Nefertari in the Valley of the Queens to teach their students hieroglyphs. Quite a distance from the days of thumbing through dry volumes of century-old hieroglyph transcriptions in a library basement!

But how to effectively employ this technology within distance learning? As always, practical experience highlights a number of issues depending on the size and geographical dispersion of the cohort. In theory, the method should be simple: tutors record 3D tours of labs, medical theatres or archaeological sites, cultural institutions or whichever other places they wish their students to visit. Using 360-degree cameras tutors can even record guided tours with audio, taking students from place to place and providing instructional commentary. Then the students view these videos or 3D photo tours with their headsets. And this is where issues arise. For one thing, it requires distance learning students to either purchase their own equipment or alternatively to receive the equipment by post or courier from the institution. This creates another level of expense either for the student or for the institution and also severely disadvantages students who live in part of the world where the postal service is less reliable or slower. Requiring students to purchase brand-new technology costing hundreds and sometimes thousands of pounds is of course not a particularly fair expense either, in particular if face-to-face students can use equipment purchased and made available on campus. Students could conceivably be asked to purchase cheaper headsets, such as those designed to work with smartphones. But again, this strategy disadvantages students from certain areas of the world where Amazon parcels are not just a click and a short wait away.

The best way to solve this issue is to use technology which functions across multiple platforms. Within the Egyptology teaching at the University of Manchester this is solved by producing 3D videos, uploading them to a hidden YouTube channel and sending the links to the students. They can then watch the video using a Google Cardboard headset or alternatively use their smartphones or even their computer screen, using the mouse to manipulate the image and "look around" their environment. As with all new technologies, of course, there is a risk that its application becomes "gimmicky", that the teaching becomes more about the method than the content or the teaching strategy.

The economic incentive for universities and other institutions in developing successful distance learning programmes is undeniable. The distance learning market has been valued at over 90 billion USD in 2019, and the trend is moving upwards. By contrast the cost of distance learning programmes can be kept relatively low. There are fewer costs associated with infrastructure, beyond staff offices, and similar and no clashing time tables. As many university libraries are already prioritising the purchase of e-books rather than physical tomes, distance learning students can access the same material as face-to-face students without ever visiting a university building, switching on a university lightbulb or wearing out a piece of university furniture. With figures like that, it is not surprising that both universities and private companies and individuals have their eyes fixed on the positive profit margins. Even a cursory Google search on the topic of "money" and "online learning" will bring up hundreds of hastily written articles with titles like "How to Make $100,000 a Year Creating Online Courses". In such a febrile environment, with so much money at stake, it is again crucial to remember that the purpose of distance learning is to broaden learner participation, to enable students from non-traditional backgrounds, mature students, students with caring responsibilities and similar to participate in high-quality education.

With the tightening of immigration policies throughout the world distance learning has become even more important. It allows the creation of a borderless teaching environment where students do not require visas wherever in the world they may be from, where they need not worry about being turned into pawns in political games, where they can learn from home, but gain the benefits of an international education and outlook and association with other students from all over the world. The internet is often vilified for the new types of crime and state control that its invention and spread has made possible. But if used properly, the internet is a foundational and transformative engine for a truly international teaching environment – not a second fiddle to traditional face-to-face teaching, but a vehicle for discourse, learning and teaching across borders, genders, ages and creeds.

Note

1 A number of peer-reviewed articles and other publications (for instance George-Palilonis and Filak 2009; Mullamaa 2010; Ahmed 2012) on distance education have attempted to trace the origins of distance education – in particular e-learning – all the way back to the Greek philosopher Plato by attributing to him the quote: "Some day, in the distant future, our grandchildren's grandchildren will develop a

Distance education 19

new equivalent of our classrooms. They will spend many hours in front of boxes with fires glowing within. May they have the wisdom to know the difference between light and knowledge." However, while this would indeed be quite a gratifying ancestral inspiration, it is also a fallacy. The quote does not appear in any of Plato's works, and in fact does not appear anywhere prior to 2006, when it was quoted in a short publication on tools for e-learning (Ramshirish and Singh 2006). Since then, it has been redeployed seemingly uncritically across a wide range of mediums, underlining the importance of rigorous source criticism in any academic discipline.

Works cited

Ahmed, P. S. (2012). The Way We Teach, the Way They Learn. *Procedia-Social and Behavioural Sciences* 47, 1554–7.
Bergmann, H. F. (2001). The Silent University: The Society to Encourage Studies at Home, 1873–1897. *The New England Quarterly* 74:3, 447–77.
Bower, B. L. and K. P. Hardy (2004). From Correspondence to Cyberspace: Changes and Challenges in Distance Education. *New Directions for Community Colleges* 2004:128, 5–12.
Boyle, F., K. Jinhee, C. Ross and O. Simpson (2010). Student–student Mentoring for Retention and Engagement in Distance Education. *Open Learning: The Journal of Open, Distance and e-Learning* 25:2, 115–30.
Caruth, G. D. and D. L. Caruth (2013). Distance Education in the United States: From Correspondence Courses to the Internet. *Turkish Online Journal of Distance Education* 14:2, 141–9.
Cunningham, K. S. (1931). *Primary Education by Correspondence: Being an Account of the Methods and Achievements of the Australian Correspondence Schools in Instructing Children Living in Isolated Areas*. Melbourne University Press: Melbourne.
Dorey, P. (2015). 'Well, Harold Insists on Having It!'—The Political Struggle to Establish the Open University, 1965–67. *Contemporary British History* 29:2, 241–72.
Gaddén, G. (1973). *Hermods 1898–1973: ett bidrag till det svenska undervisnings väsendets historia*. Hermod: Malmö.
Gaumnitz, W. H. (1952). Growth Evidence: Historical Highlights of Correspondence Education. *The Bulletin of the National Association of Secondary School Principals* 36:190, 38–46.
George-Palilonis, J. and V. Filak (2009). Blended Learning in the Visual Communications Classroom: Student Reflections on a Multimedia Course. *Electronic Journal of e-Learning* 7:3, 247–56.
Harry, K. (1992). Distance Education Today and Tomorrow: A Personal Perspective. *Educational Media International* 29:3, 189–92.
Harting, K. and M. J. Erthal (2005). History of Distance Learning. *Information Technology, Learning, and Performance Journal* 23:1, 35–44.
Heyman, E. (2010). Overcoming Student Retention Issues in Higher Education Online Programs. *Online Journal of Distance Learning Administration* 13:4.
Holmberg, B. (1995). The Evolution of the Character and Practice of Distance Education. *Open Learning: The Journal of Open, Distance and e-Learning* 10:2, 47–53.

Holmberg, B. (2005). *The Evolution, Principles and Practices of Distance Education*. BIS-Verlag: Oldenburg.

Katane, I., E. Katans and G. Vāvere (2012). Distance Education in Historical Aspect in Proceedings of the International Scientific Conference Society. Integration. Education, 312–321.

Keene, K. (2013). Blending and Flipping Distance Education. *Distance Learning* 10:4, 63–9.

Kulich, J. (1970). *An Historical Overview of the Adult Self-Learner*. British Columbia University: Vancouver.

Lederman, D. (2018). Online Education Ascends. *Inside Higher Education*, November 7th 2018. Available from: www.insidehighered.com/digital-learning/article/2018/11/07/new-data-online-enrollments-grow-and-share-overall-enrollment

McLaughlin, J. E., L. M. Griffin, D. A. Esserman, C. A. Davidson, D. M. Glatt, M. T. Roth, N. Gharkholonarehe and R. J. Mumper. (2013). Pharmacy Student Engagement, Performance, and Perception in a Flipped Satellite Classroom. *American Journal of Pharmaceutical Education* 77:9. Available from: www.ajpe.org/doi/full/10.5688/ajpe779196

Moore, P. (1995). Learning and Teaching in Virtual Worlds: Implications of Virtual Reality for Education. *Australasian Journal of Educational Technology* 11:2, 91–102.

Mullamaa, K. (2010). Going 100% on-line with Language Courses: Possible? *Journal of Language Teaching & Research* 1:5, 531–9.

n.a. (1728). Advertisement. *The Boston Gazette*, iss. 436, 2.

Neal, L. (2001). Storytelling at a Distance. *eLearn* 5, 4.

Pierrakeas, C., G. Koutsonikos, A. D. Lipitakis, S. Kotsiantis, M. Xenos and G. A. Gravvanis (2019). The Variability of the Reasons for Student Dropout in Distance Learning and the Prediction of Dropout-prone Students. In *Machine Learning Paradigms*, 91–111. Springer Basel: Basel.

Ramshirish, M. and P. Singh. (2006). E-learning: Tools and Technology. In *Proceedings for the DRTC Conference on ICT for the Digital Learning Environment*. Bangalore, 11–13.

Rickel, J. and W. L. Johnson (1998). STEVE: A Pedagogical Agent for Virtual Reality. *Agents* 98, 332–3.

Rowntree, D. (1995). Teaching and Learning Online: A Correspondence Education for the 21st Century? *British Journal of Educational Technology* 26:3, 205–15.

Simpson, O. (2003). *Student Retention in Online, Open and Distance Learning*. Routledge: Oxford.

Simpson, O. (2004). The Impact on Retention of Interventions to Support Distance Learning Students. *Open Learning: The Journal of Open, Distance and e-Learning* 19:1, 79–95.

Stacey, E. and L. Visser (2005). The History of Distance Education in Australia. *Quarterly Review of Distance Education* 6:3, 253–9.

Taylor, J. C. (1995). Distance Education Technologies: The Fourth Generation. *Australian Journal of Educational Technology* 11, 1–7.

Watkinson, J. D. (1996). Education for Success: The International Correspondence Schools of Scranton, Pennsylvania. *The Pennsylvania Magazine of History and Biography* 120:4, 343–69.

2 Beneath the bandages
Teaching Egyptology Online

Joyce Tyldesley

Five thousand years ago the Nile Valley and Delta were occupied by a series of independent city-states and their satellite communities. In 3100 BCE the southern warrior king Narmer mustered a fleet and sailed northwards, following the River Nile towards the Mediterranean Sea. Intent on conquest, he and his troops gradually persuaded the city-states to follow him, creating one long, thin realm. Narmer became the first king of the north African land that we now call Egypt. Three thousand years of dynastic rule followed during which, despite fluctuations in power and prestige, Egypt maintained a culture so distinctive that even in our modern world, it has instant recognition (Tyldesley 2005: 7).

Ancient Egypt lost and found

In 30 BCE, everything changed. Queen Cleopatra VII committed suicide and Egypt lost all independence, effectively becoming a Roman province. A second major change came in 391 CE, when Emperor Theodosius forced Egypt to become a Christian country. The compulsory abandonment of Egypt's many gods led to the closure of their temples and associated libraries – the traditional repositories of knowledge – causing the hieroglyphic inscriptions that decorated the tomb and temple walls to become unreadable. Finally, in 640 CE came the Arab conquest. Arabic was now the official language and script of Egypt, and Western visitors found it dangerous to travel south of Cairo. The writings of some Classical and Arabic authors, combined with occasional mentions in the Bible, served as a reminder of Egypt's long and complicated history, but these writings were scanty and vague and only available to scholars. Stripped of their history and largely ignored, the monuments and artefacts that littered the land could only hint at Egypt's glorious and lengthy past.

In 1798 Napoleon's invasion of Egypt led directly to the discovery of the Rosetta Stone that, in 1822, allowed the French linguist Jean-François

Champollion to crack the hieroglyphic code. Included on Napoleon's civilian staff was the *Commission des Sciences et Arts d'Égypte*, an illustrious band of scholars charged with the task of recording and publishing the natural and ancient history of Egypt. Their *Description de l'Égypte, ou, Recueil des Observations et des Recherches qui ont été faites en Égypte pendant l'expédition de l'armée français, publié par les ordres de Sa Majesté l'empereur Napoléon le Grand* was eventually published as nine volumes of text and 11 volumes of plates (1809–29); a subsequent 24 volume re-issue (1820–30) included five volumes devoted to antiquities. The *Description* opened Western eyes to Egypt's ancient art and architecture, sparking a craze for a romanticised "Nile-style" which has continued to the present day (Moreno Garcia 2015). Films, books and documentaries about ancient Egypt – fact and fiction – are perennially popular, as are Egypt-themed museum displays. Ancient Egyptian design inspires fashion, jewellery, architecture, body art and advertising, while devotees, drawn to what they see as the "spirituality" of the past, follow modern versions of the ancient cults that the Egyptians themselves would struggle to recognise. Effectively, ancient Egypt has become isolated from its ancient neighbours and in many ways separated from reality too, so that in the popular imagination it flourishes as if in a sanitised bubble, entirely separate from the world around it – a bubble filled with beautiful art, beautiful buildings and beautiful people which, for many, offers an escape from the often harsh realities of modern daily life.

From a pedagogic perspective, it is important that Egyptology teachers recognise this wealth of unofficial and unregulated information, as everyone who undertakes a more formal study of ancient Egypt will be to a certain extent self-taught, having pulled together a personal, informal programme of readings, television documentaries, internet resources etc. These students may need to spend some time confronting and unlearning the errors, assumptions and expectations picked up from popular culture. To take a trivial example: the fact that the 1999 film *The Mummy* makes specific reference to five canopic jars rather than four (the correct number) may seem unimportant, but colleagues can confirm that this error has been repeated in university exam scripts many, many times. A more serious example is provided by the surprising number of students taught by the author in different learning environments over many years who have confided that they never imagined that there was crime in ancient Egypt. It is necessary that these issues are addressed in a tactful and non-judgemental way; students who have their beliefs shattered too abruptly are prone to dig their heels in, and stop learning before they have really started. Online students, who may feel little attachment to their remote learning institution and who have not made the same commitments to their studies as face-to-face learners – they are unlikely to have given up employment and relocated their families, for example – are particularly prone to abandon courses which, for whatever reason, do not meet their expectations. This "distance learning deficit" results in many online courses having less than a quarter of the graduation rate of more traditionally taught courses (statistic discussed by Simpson 2013). This high rate of attrition tends to be ignored at the institutional level until student numbers reach a tipping point, a course becomes financially unviable, and it is closed.

Much of the Egyptology teaching strategy outlined in this book is focused on making students feel as comfortable as possible in their learning environment. We want our students to feel as at home at the University of Manchester, as familiar with our teaching staff, as connected to fellow students, as confident using the library and as welcome "visiting" the museum as the face-to-face students do, if not more so. We know that some students will have to leave our courses due to unforeseen problems (ill health, financial problems, caring responsibilities etc) but we want to reduce the numbers who drop out for less obviously valid reasons. This approach – which at its most basic level is simple, old-fashioned courtesy – leads to increased student engagement and a happy working environment that benefits both students and staff.

Teaching Egyptology in Britain

Egyptology may be broadly defined as "the disciplined study of ancient Egypt" (Carruthers 2015: 1). This is a vast umbrella, covering more than 5,000 years of archaeology, language studies, history, social history, science, art, religion, technology, mummy studies and much more. While the earlier Egyptologists attempted to do everything – excavate a site, translate its inscriptions, analyse its material culture and even autopsy its mummies – today professional Egyptologists specialise in one or two of these areas, or excavate just one archaeological site for many years. They are team players rather than hero archaeologists working in splendid isolation. Those who teach ancient Egyptian history tend to confine their syllabus to the history of the dynastic or pharaonic period between Narmer's unification and the death of Cleopatra, with some also including the Predynastic period immediately preceding unification and others including the time post-Cleopatra, when Rome ruled Egypt.

Egyptologists may study an ancient civilisation, but Egyptology itself is a modern academic subject unrecognised, or at least unnamed, before the 1860s (Champion 2003: 180; Stevenson 2015: 30 note 1). Prior to 1822, the ancient Egyptian artefacts which made their way into Western museums and private collections had no real context; they were attractive but essentially meaningless curiosities. The decipherment of the hieroglyphic script allowed linguists to translate and publish the ancient texts. Chronologies were developed, time-lines devised, and dynastic history slowly emerged, allowing Egypt's hitherto confusing archaeology to be slotted into its proper context. Egyptology became an academically respectable subject worthy of teaching at university level (Stevenson 2015: 21).

In 1892 Flinders Petrie became the Edwards Professor of Egyptian Archaeology and Philology (Janssen 1992). His chair, the first Egyptology chair in Britain, was funded by a legacy from the novelist Amelia B. Edwards and based at University College London, because Miss Edwards objected to the fact that Oxford and Cambridge refused to admit women to degrees. Today the UK offers taught Egyptology or Egyptian archaeology programmes at the Universities of Cambridge, Liverpool, London, Manchester, Oxford and Swansea, with several other universities offering taught programmes that include a significant Egyptology component (usually archaeology, ancient history or ancient world programmes). The same universities offer research degrees in Egyptology or Egyptian archaeology. In addition, some UK universities offer Egyptology courses through their "Continuing Education" or similarly named extramural departments, where students may enrol on a wide range of flexible credit-bearing or non-credit-bearing units but do not necessarily study for a degree, are not always taught by the university lecturers, and do not mix with students on the formal degree programmes. Finally, as part of their commitment to outreach and accessibility, some universities and museums offer free online education, ranging from occasional lectures, to Massive Online Open Courses (MOOCs), while others offer occasional study days open to all who apply.

Despite its general popularity, Egyptology remains a small and specialised UK university discipline in comparison with many other humanities subjects. Because it is not taught in schools, Egyptology is not an immediately obvious choice of degree: students have to actively seek it out. Students (and their parents) who are initially interested in studying ancient Egypt may regretfully decide that it is an expensive dead end when compared to a vocational degree. This is unfair. The limited job market means that very few Egyptology students will find work as professional Egyptologists, but the discipline offers a wealth of transferable skills (including, amongst others, the study of language, history, geography, theology and art; effective time management; the creation of one or more sustained and original pieces of work) which make it comparable in terms of employability with more traditional humanities subjects such as Latin, Greek, archaeology and ancient history.

Outside the university and museum system, UK Egyptology is taught face-to-face via traditional night school courses run by educational institutions such as the Worker's Education Association, the University of the

Third Age and various further education collages. Societies and commercial organisations organise lectures, study days and study weeks taught by visiting Egyptologists, while travel companies offer the experience of visiting the ancient sites in the company of an expert. The internet offers online Egyptology courses of variable quality and content, taught by a wide range of "experts". Egyptology is not currently taught at secondary school level, but it does form an optional part of the national curriculum for primary schools in England (Key Stage 2: see Chapter 7).

Teaching Egyptology at the University of Manchester

The Manchester Museum, part of the University of Manchester, houses a large and important collection of ancient Egyptian artefacts, many of which were donated by local businessman Jesse Haworth from 1890 to 1921 (Alberti 2009: 71, 171). Initially the museum, which was primarily a natural history museum, was reluctant to accept his collection: it was felt that ancient Egypt was a subject of neither scholarly nor general interest. When Haworth offered to donate sufficient money to build an extension to the building, there was rapid change of policy. Egyptian artefacts were welcomed into the museum, and today the Egyptology gallery is one of its most popular attractions, rivalled only by the museum's dinosaurs. As many of the artefacts are provenanced, having been acquired directly from Petrie's excavations, they form an excellent teaching collection. Unfortunately, as is often the case, spatial limitations ensure that only a small percentage of the artefacts can be on public display.

The Egyptology galleries required a dedicated keeper or curator of Egyptology. During the 1970s, this curator was Dr Rosalie David. Dr David not only worked at the museum, specialising in mummy studies, she also taught an Egyptology evening class for the University's Centre for Continuing Education. This class was to evolve into the first programme of the University's current suite of online Egyptology programmes and learning experiences. The various stages of this development are as follows:

1970–2004: face-to-face and postal teaching

Egyptology was not taught at undergraduate or postgraduate level at the University of Manchester, but it was taught as an evening class via the Centre for Continuing Education. The programme, which had an intake every four years, consisted of three taught years plus one year of independent study. Students completing the programme were awarded a "Certificate", which was defined as 120 credits: 60 credits at Level 1 (broadly equivalent to the level of first year undergraduate study) and 30 credits at each of Levels 2 (second year undergraduate study) and 3 (third year undergraduate

26   Joyce Tyldesley

study) (Gill 2007: 23). This definition of a "Certificate" does not match the standard definition of a university Certificate of Higher Education or CertHE, which expects 120 credits at Level 1 (first year of undergraduate study). Students who complete the first year of an undergraduate degree and do not go on to a second year are awarded a Certificate of Higher Education.

The face-to-face programme was eventually transformed into a distance learning course, making it accessible to a wider student base, including those unable to travel to Manchester. This new course was paper based, with teaching materials (monthly booklets, a video tape of photographs with a voice-over commentary, and three short films specially produced for the course on video: *Daily Life in Ancient Egypt, Funerary Beliefs and Customs* and *Looking at Museum Objects*) distributed by post. Students were required to complete monthly written assignments: these were marked and returned to the student by a team of tutors. Tutors might also discuss work with students by telephone. The face-to-face Certificate course ran alongside the postal version.

2004–7: the creation of an online course

In 2004, in recognition of the increasing number of home computers connected to the internet, the decision was taken to move the postal Certificate course online. It was not envisaged that every student would have access to a private computer, but it was expected that those who could not study from home would be able to use the facilities provided by public libraries and internet cafes. The move offered the major advantages of decreased administrative and postal costs while allowing increased accessibility to students worldwide. From a pedagogic viewpoint, it allowed increased student–student, student–tutor and tutor–tutor contact, improving the student experience and decreasing the feelings of isolation occasionally reported in feedback on the postal course.

This remodelling of the postal and face-to-face courses has been described in some detail by Gill, who worked alongside a project manager, members of the Centre for Continuing Education, course tutors, and members of the University's Distributed Learning (DL) Unit to facilitate the change (2007). Funding and support were obtained from the DL Unit, and the Unit's graphic designer created a design for the course homepage and icons.

The course that emerged was hosted on the University's Virtual Learning Environment, WebCT. A shared home page allowed all registered students access to a shared discussion area, a shared study skills and technical help area, the course handbook and one of four specific year groups:

- Year 1: Predynastic Egypt to the Reign of the Hyksos
- Year 2: The 18th Dynasty

- Year 3: The 19th Dynasty to the Arab Conquest
- Year 4: Dissertation

A calendar tool provided information on dates for the release of modules and assignment deadlines, and there was a glossary of frequently encountered names and terms linking into the text. There were two assignments in each of the first two years plus a Year 4 dissertation of 10,000 words. The course was taught by a team of experienced Egyptologists with varying degrees of computer literacy, all based off campus. These tutors were allocated to discussion groups on a rota basis.

Within each year group there were eight timed-release units, each made up of three or four text-based learning modules plus a discussion area used to present weekly activities. The learning modules were created from the repurposed postal and face-to-face course notes and illustrated with images scanned and uploaded from Dr David's slide collection. They relied heavily on a database of themed pages, accessed via links within the text. Effectively, each page of text functioned in the same way that a Wikipedia page functions, with background information supplemented by links to pages of more specific information plus links to a glossary for short definitions. As well as selected database pages being accessible within each learning module, the entire database was available to students via a link in WebCT.

2007: the creation of a faculty compliant programme

By September 2007, the online Certificate course was running with, for the first time, students in all four years. When the decision was taken to close the Centre for Continuing Education (now known as Courses for the Public), Dr David, now Professor David, was able to save the Certificate by negotiating a transfer into the newly formed KNH Centre for Biomedical Egyptology, a part of the Faculty of Life Sciences (FLS). Dr Joyce Tyldesley was appointed to organise, administer, teach and develop the next phase of the Certificate programme.

The move to the more formal structure of the FLS necessitated immediate changes to the Certificate programme if it was to both comply with faculty regulations and become financially viable. The changes started with the simplification of the teaching structure. The team of tutors had by now grown to ten, working in pairs on a rota system. This was an expensive and unwieldy system for a Level 1 programme with fewer than 100 students. There were issues over the handover of work (if a student posted late to the discussion board, who should reply, the old team or the new?) and confusion over course ownership (who, exactly, was responsible for reviewing and updating the learning modules?). The students were lacking a sense of continuity and personal connection as their tutors changed on a regular basis. Dr Tyldesley took over all teaching duties as programme tutor, working in close co-operation with a course administrator and the faculty eLearning team. From 2008 funds were made available to employ a dedicated hieroglyphs tutor. As Manchester's online provision has grown, this temporary post has gradually become a full-time position. Initially this post was held by Dr Glenn Godenho; now it is held by Dr Nicky Nielsen. In 2019 an additional part-time hieroglyphs tutor joined the team.

From the outset it was decided that the programme tutor would be responsible for the entire teaching and learning process – designing, writing and editing the course material, uploading the course material, creating quizzes, assignments and discussions, and working with students on the discussion boards. The eLearning department would offer support to both staff and students as necessary but would not be involved in the day-to-day running of the programme.

One important aspect of the old Certificate course that was retained was the principle of open entry. Certificate students are not required to have a sustained history of formal education. Indeed, a significant number of our students left school aged 16 or younger in times and places when a university education was only available to a privileged few. One of our current students speaks for many when writing "I left school when I was 14. If it were not for distance learning I wouldn't have any academic qualifications at all" (Anonymous, 2019). Data from the Office for National Statistics shows that overall participation in higher education has increased from 3.4% in 1950 to 33% in 2000 (Bolton 2012: 14). In 1980, the year prior to my graduation, only 68,150 students obtained UK university degrees. In 2011 there were 350,800 graduates.

We are committed to the principle that "everyone with the potential to benefit from Higher Education should have equal opportunity to do so" (National Strategy for Access and Student Success in Higher Education 2014). These atypical students bring a lifetime of valuable experiences to our programmes, and we would never want to lose them. In place of exam grades, all applicants are required to demonstrate an ability to access and use computer technology at a basic level (familiarity with creating and uploading a Word document) and an ability to work comfortably and fluently in English, the language of the course. The application process therefore requires students to download a form, fill it in, and write two short submissions of between 300 and 500 words.

2008–9: remodelling the certificate programme

A move from the WebCT to Blackboard platform prompted a complete rewrite of the Certificate, making it fully faculty compliant. The four years of the programme were given individual course codes so that there was effectively a separate Blackboard for each year of the programme, accessible only to students within that year. This was a non-negotiable faculty decision, which threatened the sense of cross-year community that had developed on the shared WebCT board. In response, to allow the students in different years to continue to communicate easily with each other, "Community" was created as a shared staff-student area providing discussion boards, learning resources and general course information.

Hieroglyph-based icons created by the eLearning team were used throughout the programme and its advertising in order to promote a shared sense of unity, identity and recognition amongst students spread throughout the world. This "branding" would later be extended to cover the use of introductory music and graphics in videos, podcasts and vlogs and the use of colour-coding to distinguish between the various programmes. Its importance as a means of allowing students to feel a sense of "belonging" should not be underestimated but is difficult to measure, as few of our students have experience of other, unbranded on line courses.

Within the three taught years of the Certificate, the inconsistently sized units were remodelled to create seven consecutive topics, each with four learning modules of equivalent size, taught at Level 1. Effectively, there was now one learning module per week. Each new learning module consisted of written text with updated illustrations and hyperlinks to external resources (museums, websites and reading material), plus a discussion activity that would generate work to be shared on a tutorial discussion board. Gradually, as technology allowed, recorded lectures were added to the learning modules and the amount of written text was decreased. The database, which had grown unwieldy and was already significantly outdated, was eliminated, and the glossary was removed. A fixed calendar was introduced with topics opening on the first day of each month, making it easy for students with busy lives to remember important course dates.

The uneven nature of the syllabus – thousands of years of history covered in Years 1 and 3; just one dynasty covered in far greater detail in Year 2 – was addressed by adding aspects of art, religion, technology and social history to Year 2. In hindsight it would have been better to have completely revised the syllabus, redesigning each of the three years from scratch. But the requirement to change all three years simultaneously with very little notice (due to the imposed move from WebCT to Blackboard) made this impossible. In the future it is intended to address this issue.

Year 4, with its requirement to research and write a 10,000-word dissertation, posed a huge problem. Most university teachers would agree that is an excessively ambitious requirement for a Level 1 programme or first-year equivalent student. In comparison, for example, a UK master's programme (Level 4) usually carries the requirement to research and write a

Figure 2.1 Certificate Programme Icons

15–20,000-word dissertation. The dissertation was therefore dropped from the Certificate, which was reduced to a three-year (part-time) programme of 40 credits per year taught at Level 1. To avoid complaints from students who had initially registered for a four-year course and who specifically wanted to write a dissertation, three- and four-year versions of the course ran in parallel for two years, with students able to select their own pathway. Several availed themselves of the opportunity to spend a year researching ancient Egypt, even though this extra year did not carry any additional credit.

The Certificate programme currently attracts an average of 35 students per year, with student retention consistently high. Students are drawn from many countries, with the highest numbers coming from the United

Kingdom, the United States and Australia. A high percentage of our students have English as their second or third language.

2010: Short Courses in Egyptology

In 2010 Short Courses in Egyptology was launched in response to a growing student-led demand for more online Egyptology. Short Courses runs in October and May each year, offering a choice of themed courses, each six weeks long, plus two opening weeks of introductory material and course orientation and two final weeks without formal teaching to finish any outstanding activity work. As this is a non-credit-bearing programme, there are no graded assessments. In a normal year, 100+ students will experience Short Courses, with several progressing from one option to the next until all have been completed.

Short Courses in Egyptology is primarily aimed at:

- Students contemplating joining the Certificate programme but worried that they or their computer equipment might not be able to cope with the necessary technology.
- Students contemplating joining the Certificate programme who have been out of the education system for some time.
- Students registered for the Certificate programme and waiting for it to start.
- Students who have finished the Certificate programme who wish to continue studying with the University of Manchester.
- Students who for financial, geographical, physical or other reasons are unable to register for the Certificate programme.
- Tourists wishing to prepare for a trip to Egypt.

By retaining the same teaching team, learning module, activity and discussion board structure as the Certificate programme, and by keeping the price appropriately low, Short Courses became an effective taster course for the Certificate programme with three or four students each year progressing from Short Courses to the Certificate. Here one student speaks for many (2019):

> I selected this particular course [the Certificate] because I tried the taster courses and enjoyed the material, instructors, and teaching style. It allowed me to sample the classes before making a time and financial commitment for further studies.

The value of Short Courses was confirmed when the faculty unexpectedly and without consultation imposed a 100% price increase to bring Short Courses in Egyptology in line with the university's medical Continuing Professional Development courses. Enrolment plummeted both on Short

Courses and, after a time lag, on the Certificate. The old price structure was quickly restored, but it took three years for both programmes to regain their previous student numbers.

Currently there are seven Short Courses options on offer: these may be taken consecutively, or two or more together:

- Queens of Ancient Egypt
- Gods and Goddesses of Ancient Egypt
- Tutankhamen
- Discovering Ancient Egypt
- Hieroglyphs I
- Hieroglyphs II
- Hieroglyphs III

2011–18: Egyptology Online

The growing popularity of the online Egyptology courses prompted the creation of Egyptology Online: a virtual centre of online excellence entirely independent of the KNH Centre for Biomedical Egyptology. To support Egyptology Online, a dedicated website was created: www.alc.manchester.ac.uk/egyptology/research/. This has evolved over the years to incorporate free lectures, details of online courses, podcasts and a blog. It is now an important part of our recruitment strategy, the entry point at which many students first encounter the University of Manchester and the place where students access the enrolment portal for the Certificate, Diploma and Short Courses programmes. A Twitter account and a monthly newsletter also encourage potential students to consider studying at the University of Manchester. At the other end of the spectrum, a Facebook group – *The Two Crowns* – offers a discussion forum for ex-students who wish to remain in contact with students and staff.

In 2011 the online Diploma in Egyptology was launched. This two-year part-time programme offers 120 credits at Level 2 (the second year of an undergraduate degree in the UK); together with the Certificate programme it creates a Diploma in Egyptology bearing a total of 240 credits. Unlike the Certificate programme, the Diploma was designed from scratch, in line with faculty requirements. It was therefore possible to create a programme of ten consecutive units, taught following the teaching methods refined on the Certificate programme. This time, the course icons were gold (although on some computer monitors they appear a rather unlovely orange colour).

Year 1

- Social Life in Middle Kingdom Egypt: Kahun: 10 credits
- Social Life in New Kingdom Egypt: Deir el-Medina: 10 credits

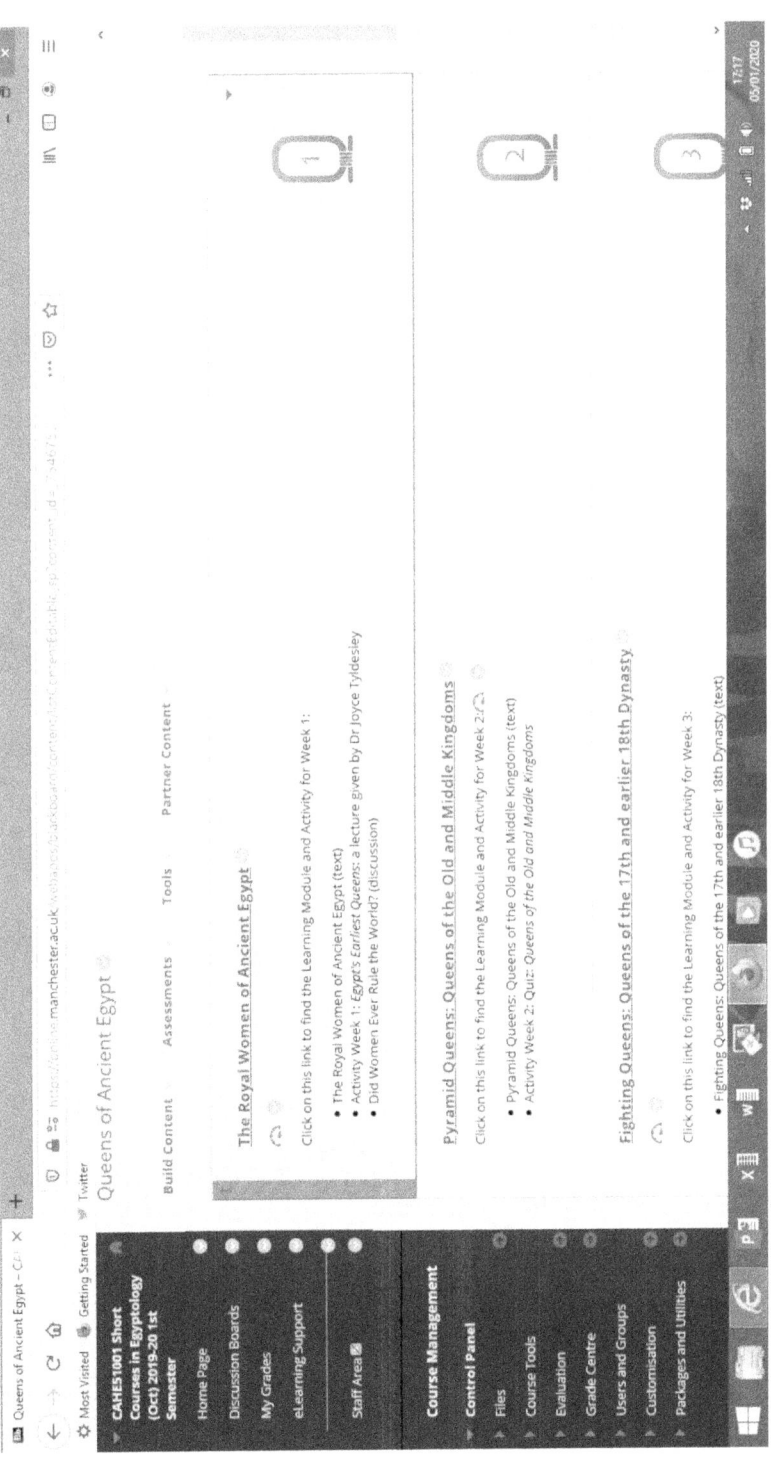

Figure 2.2 Short Courses: Screenshot showing weekly learning modules for Queens of Ancient Egypt. The discussion boards are accessed via the left-hand menu.

- Egyptian Technology I: Manipulating the Natural World: 10 credits
- Egyptian Technology II: Pyrotechnology: 10 credits
- Tombs and Tomb Owners: 20 credits

Year 2

- Scientific Approaches to Egyptian Problems: 10 credits
- Towns and Cities: 10 credits
- Understanding Egyptian Texts I: 10 credits
- Understanding Egyptian Texts II: 10 credits
- Egypt and Nubia: 20 credits

The Diploma has been consistently popular, attracting an average of 15 students per year.

Having developed the Diploma programme, Egyptology Online worked in close cooperation with the FLS e-Learning team to create a suite of freely available online Egyptology-themed resources. These outreach activities allowed experimentation with new formats, new platforms and new student audiences while serving as adverts and taster courses for the formal, income-generating programmes. This work will be discussed in more detail in Chapters 6 and 7. At the same time, there was experimentation within the formal programmes; this included the creation of photobooks, short videos recorded in the stores of the Manchester Museum and self-assessed hieroglyphic worksheets. In 2012, funded by a Teaching Innovations grant, Dr Tyldesley travelled to Egypt to take a series of photographs and short videos to incorporate in the programmes.

2019: the MA in Egyptology

It was envisaged that, with the Diploma up and running, a third "tier" (two years part-time, taught at Level 3) would be added to the Certificate and Diploma, creating the world's first online degree in Egyptology. However, this proposal threw up several unforeseen administrative difficulties concerning examinations and progression, which are still waiting to be resolved. Instead, it was suggested that it might be easier to implement an online MA, as this would be a stand-alone programme that could be examined entirely by coursework. This would create a suite of separate but linked online programmes and learning environments that would allow students to flow from informal learning to a formal learning programme entirely within the system.

In September 2019 Egyptology Online moved to the Humanities Faculty at the University of Manchester, becoming an integral part of the newly formed Department of Classics, Ancient History, Archaeology and Egyptology. At the same time, an online MA in Egyptology (two years, part-time,

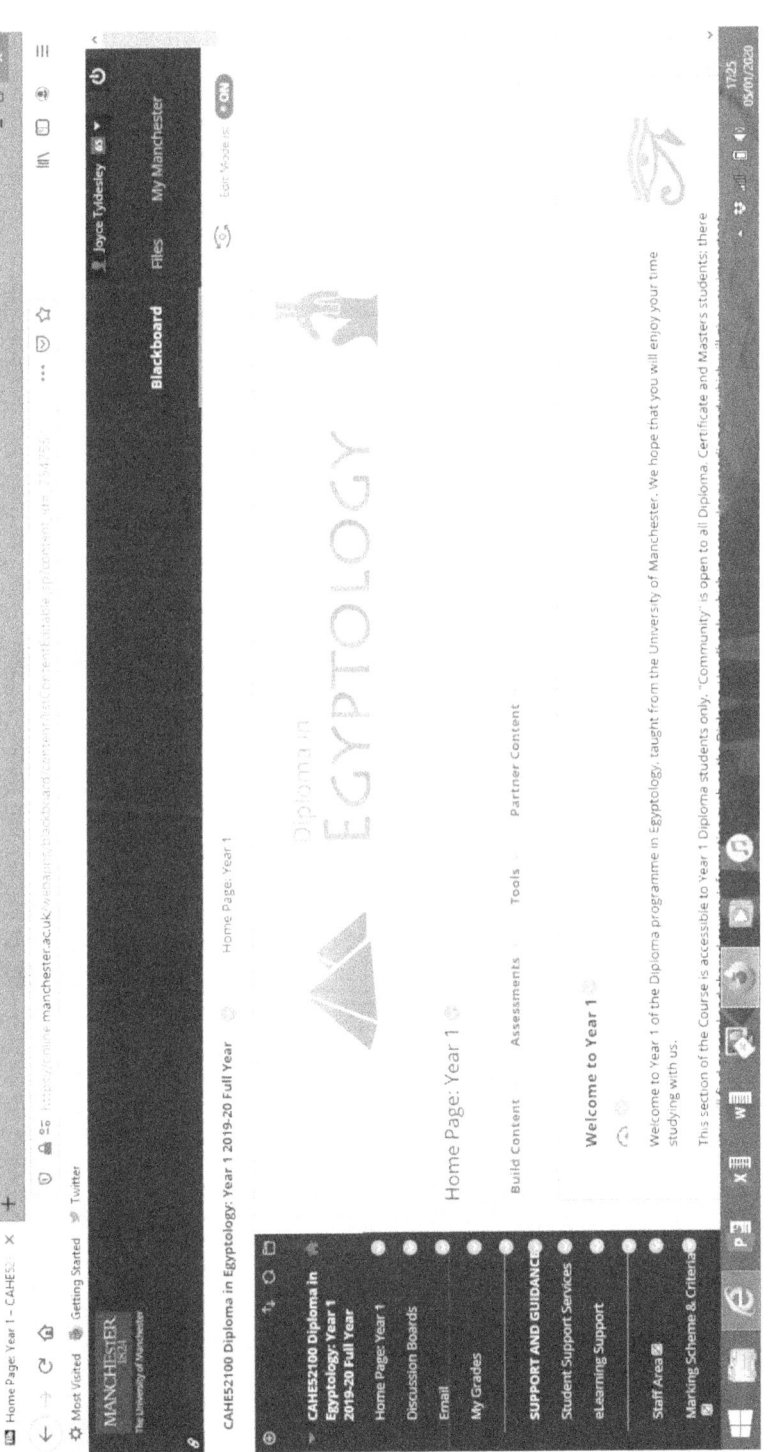

Figure 2.3 The Diploma Programme Home Page: Site of the units and learning modules

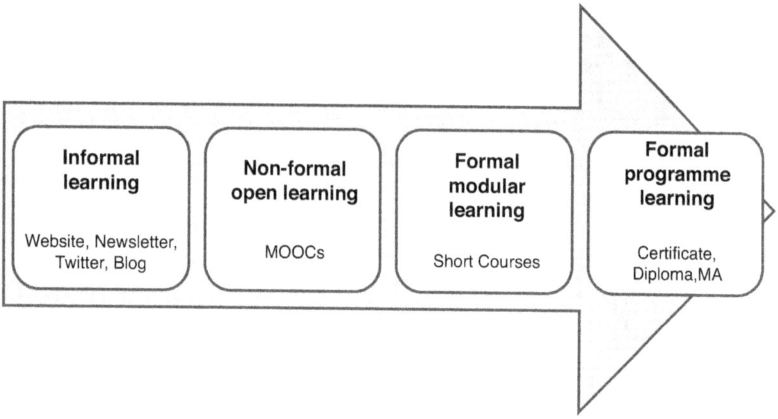

```
Informal learning          Non-formal open learning    Formal modular learning    Formal programme learning
Website, Newsletter,       MOOCs                       Short Courses              Certificate,
Twitter, Blog                                                                     Diploma, MA
```

Figure 2.4 A Linked System of Online Programmes and Learning Experiences

180 credits at Level 4) was launched with an initial intake of 39 students. The MA employs the teaching techniques developed for the Certificate and the Diploma programmes and already explained in this chapter. But as the MA is taught at a higher level to experienced students, there is a decreased reliance on closely directed tutor-led teaching and far more student-led research and group work. To reflect this shift of emphasis, the text within the weekly learning modules has been removed and replaced by lectures, podcasts and vlogs. All reading resources are provided within the course by the University of Manchester library, allowing students in under-resourced circumstances to study on an equal footing to their better-resourced fellow students. The hieroglyphic course icons have once again changed colour and are now purple (blue for Certificate, gold for Diploma and green for Short Courses).

The syllabus is as follows:

Year 1

Semester 1

- Academic Skills and Research Design in Egyptian Archaeology Part 1 (30 credits)
- Historical Studies in Ancient Egypt (15 credits)

Semester 2

- Academic Skills and Design in Egyptian Archaeology Part 2 (15 credits)

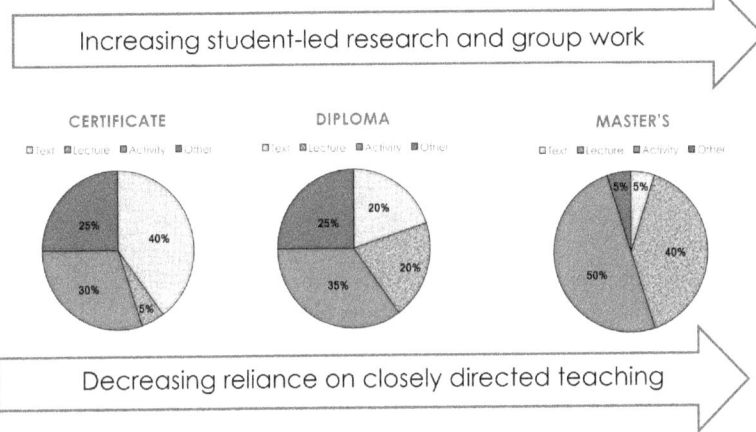

Figure 2.5 Changing learning environments across the credit-bearing programmes

- Art and Artists in Ancient Egypt (15 credits)
- Urbanism in Ancient Egypt (15 credits)

Year 2

Semester 1
Two optional units selected from:

- Ancient Egyptian Religion and Funerary Beliefs (15 credits)
- Gender and Identity in Ancient Egypt (15 credits)
- The Amarna Period (15 credits)
- Fast-track Middle Egyptian (15 credits)

Semester 2

- Dedicated to researching and writing a 15,000-word dissertation (60 credits)

It is too early to comment on the success or otherwise of the MA programme, but student feedback to date has been very positive.

The Egyptology Online student profile

So far this brief history of online Egyptology at the University of Manchester has more or less ignored the people who have the clearest view of, and the greatest investment in, the programmes under discussion. It seems fitting that the last word in this chapter is left to the people whose loyalty, and willingness to provide detailed feedback year after year has been instrumental in the development of the Manchester online teaching strategies.

Definitions of the "mature student" vary. In the UK the term is usually applied to students over the age of 21. Almost all the Manchester online Egyptology students fall into this category, with the majority being substantially older. Worldwide, the numbers of mature students in higher education is significant and rising (Ennis et al. 2017: 2). Our students' ages at registration have ranged from under 15 to 75+, with the majority falling into the 45–60 age bracket. In 2017 the average age across the Certificate and Diploma courses was 52; in 2019 it was 49. It is anticipated that this will gradually drop as the newly established online MA in Egyptology starts to attract younger students graduating from face-to-face programmes at other institutions. As student average age drops, new students are increasingly familiar with online technology, and their expectations from online teaching are correspondingly higher.

Mature students enter higher education for various reasons, including career development, the replacing of redundant skill sets and the desire to provide a role model for children (Ennis et al. 2017: 1). The vast majority of our students are those who have spent much of their working lives in "sensible" occupations and who, now approaching retirement, relish the opportunity to return to their first love: ancient Egypt. These students bring a vast wealth of experience and knowledge; they have the potential to make a valid contribution to academic Egyptology, and indeed our past students have gone on to publish books and articles, edit Egyptology magazines, work on excavations, and enrol on master's and PhD programmes.

These students have requirements that are not always apparent, particularly when the learners themselves are "invisible" online. Research indicates that mature students in general are more likely to be from lower socioeconomic status backgrounds, have caring responsibilities, be disabled and be from black and minority ethnic groups. (McVitty and Morris 2012: 4). They tend to be highly motivated and do not show the reluctance to engage with teaching staff that traditional undergraduates often display. Traditionally these students find it difficult to integrate into the university system and struggle to make valid connections with younger students (Ennis et al. 2017: 3).

Age anxiety – the feeling of being conspicuously different to everyone else in the room – is a less significant issue on online programmes, where age (and every other personal characteristic) is hidden unless the student him/herself chooses to disclose it. The Manchester Egyptology students, having chosen to study what many would classify as an expensive "hobby" subject with little or no expectation or requirement of enhanced employability and requiring access to expensive computer equipment, are more likely to have above-average incomes for their country. Feedback collected over ten years shows that they often:

- worry that they will not cope with online technology,
- are carers for children/grandchildren, partners and parents (in some cases, all three) and
- have unavoidable personal commitments (jobs, financial pressures, personal health issues).

This fits with the "risk landscape" identified by Kearns, who cites Leonard's findings that mature students are often at greater risk financially, socially, psychologically and academically than their younger counterparts (2014: 95). The Manchester students tend to exhibit excellent time-management skills but require a flexible approach, in terms of syllabus and curriculum reinforced by frequent positive feedback, to obtain the best results from their learning. They respond particularly well to an interactive and collaborative learning environment and to problem-based learning. Sensitive to criticism, they are unlikely to accept tutor feedback without questioning it. The curriculum design, teaching methods and assessments (formative and summative) and feedback mechanisms developed by Egyptology Online were designed to aid these learners while also proving entirely appropriate to younger students.

Introversion is normal for a large percentage of the population. It should not be a barrier to success, as it so often is in communities (including universities) that place great value on the "extrovert ideal" for both staff and students (Cain 2012: 4–5). Many of the Egyptology Online students have reported introvert tendencies, shyness and social anxiety. These students feel more comfortable working in a virtual rather than real classroom. They recognise that face-to-face teaching is often inadvertently biased towards the more extrovert students, with strong emphasis on obvious participation within the classroom. Group work, for these students, is very difficult. This is a phenomenon that needs to be recognised and addressed within the virtual teaching environment. To take one, extreme, example of student feedback (2019):

> Particular advantages [sic] for me is the anononimity [sic]. I suffer with anxiety and very low self esteem and this was an opportunity to grow in strength when I can see and or view my achievements. Unfortunately, I stood out as a teen, being quiet, arty and studious – I had no interest in the things my peers were doing. For this I was misunderstood, and

I got bullied. A lot. My work suffered, and my school wasn't effective at dealing with the problems, or with supporting me. When I was around 18 I got regularly beaten up in the street, and ended up having a nervous breakdown. It took me YEARS to recover. I became a frightened recluse, and so I quit college. Through this all, I never fully gave up on my dreams, and one day whilst becoming familiar with the online world of Egyptology, I found out about the online courses run by the University of Manchester. I work full time, and it was always my dream to enter academia, and study Egyptology, ancient history, learn and read the ancient texts that I knew of. I had been avidly reading everything I could on Egypt all my adult life, so this course had made it possible for me to come back to academic study, and follow what was my original vision that has stayed in my heart since I was a 12 year old. . . . Thank you to the University of Manchester for helping get a second chance.

With students distributed throughout the world Egyptology Online works with different time zones, different broadband strengths, different access to equipment and websites, different prior learning experiences and different expectations. This challenge has been met by the development and implementation of teaching strategies that, entirely asynchronous, revolves around weekly discussion board "Activities". A rigorous rolling system of feedback collection, reflection and innovation has allowed our programmes to develop from year to year.

Our students say

Student feedback is immensely useful both for the personal development of the teaching team and for programme development. It brings further, hidden benefits. By allowing our students to influence programme developments we give them a sense of ownership and belonging to a university that might actually be many hundreds of miles from their home. This positive message creates a strong bond with the programme and its teachers, and this in turn enhances the learning environment for both students and staff. Instead of feeling remote and isolated, our worldwide students feel that they have a real role to play in the development of Egyptology teaching at the University of Manchester.

Feedback is submitted formally on an annual basis through the University of Manchester appraisal questionnaire, but this feedback is too generic and too face-to-face focused to be of much use in improving and developing online teaching strategies. More useful – because it is both more detailed and more specific to our programmes – is the feedback collected each year by the Student Representatives. This is done by email, in whatever format the representatives select. Students are encouraged to comment on any and every aspect of their programme. The responses are collated by the Student Representatives and presented at the Egyptology staff-student liaison meeting.

Equally useful is the feedback submitted to Community via open but anonymous discussion boards in response to specific questions asked by the teaching staff. We have used this method to test new forms of information presentation, to discuss specific issues and to ask for suggestions for new Short Courses. The feedback received has been invaluable in showing us what will work and what will probably not work. Ideas presented and discussed this way have made their way into the course. Ideas that have been tried and rejected include the provision of a real-time student-led discussion club which started well but quickly faltered; this has been replaced by an asynchronous discussion board-based Journal Club, which continues to flourish. The asynchronous nature of all our programmes is a deliberate choice to ensure that learning is available to everyone at the time when they personally feel best able to learn. It is one that students occasionally challenge – typically one or two students in each intake will express a preference for more "live" experiences – but each time we have introduced an experimental element of real time into our programmes, they have failed amidst complaints that having to be online at a specified time is inconvenient. Our one exception to asynchronous teaching is the Skype interview that we offer to each of our MA students prior to starting their dissertation.

In preparation for this book, a dedicated discussion board was used to ask for student feedback on specific issues. Students could, if they wished, give their feedback anonymously, but only three out of over 200 responses were submitted this way. Presented here are three of the questions asked plus a sample of the responses, chosen not at random but because they raise issues which are likely to be of interest to online teachers in other institutions and other disciplines:

Question 1: Why did you decide to study on an online course? How did you select your course – what was important to you?

All answers mentioned the benefits of flexibility of online learning; lack of access to a brick and mortar library was cited as the main disadvantage.

Answer 1: When I first decided to pursue an education in Egyptology I knew it would have to be an online course. Where I lived and my life schedule made it impossible for me to do seat time at any school. When I searched for an online course on the subject the U of M courses were the first ones to come up. After looking over the available courses I decided to try the short courses first to see if it would be a good fit for me. Obviously it was because here I am four years later still loving every minute of the experience.

Answer 2: From a personal perspective I have wanted to study Egyptology since primary school after seeing an image of the Eye of Horus and was hooked (I am 41 now). I unfortunately listened to advice and did not follow my heart studying chemistry, then getting married, requalifying with H&S and now divorced it is my time to reset the clock :-)

Answer 3: For me a long distance course was the only option as I was working at the time and I would be able to fit it around work and other interests. Also with my particular health issues attending classes regularly at a campus, unless evenings, would have been problematic. I already knew people who had done the course and had enjoyed it and that it was interactive through the discussion boards so that I would not feel isolated.

Answer 4: I picked a distance learning Egyptology course because I'd always wanted to complete a degree of some sort in Egyptology, but I'd never been at a college/university that offered it as a degree option. I'm at a point in my life where I can't quit my day job to attend school full time, so I wanted something part time and preferably online. I did some online research and came across the University of Manchester program. I believe I watched one of the free symposia before applying. It's important to me when taking an online course that the instructors communicate effectively using the available online tools. I have to say that I'm glad I applied and was accepted to the program.

Answer 5: I have always loved to study and when I stumbled across a learning course that incorporated my love of Egypt it just had to be done which is why I am here. A particular advantage for me is the anononimity. I suffer with anxiety and very low self esteem and this was an opportunity to grow in strength when I can see and or view my achievements. The disadvantages are the dangers of lack of self motivation. I feel when you are in a visual class group you can help motivate each other and views/comments are not as easily misinterpreted.

Answer 6: I picked this distance learning course for several reasons. A few years ago, I attended a post-graduate certificate course at a local university and found the hours inconvenient for riding public transport safely, the facilities sub-standard (broken chairs, toilets locked after 6 p.m.), and the whole thing inflexible. After taking early retirement, I wanted to do something intellectually challenging, and after doing a series of MOOCs, found that the majority scratched the surface of their subject but left little opportunity to continue. Then I found the Manchester Egyptology short courses and re-discovered my long-abandoned interest in ancient Egypt. I have been a happy student since then. The course work can be done at my convenience, it is in-depth and challenging, and the continuity of tutors and students over the three-year certificate course has provided stability. I enjoy working with others from around the globe in a wonderfully diverse student group.

Question 2: Have you or anyone you know ever thought/suggested that a distance learning qualification is less valid than a qualification obtained by face-to-face teaching? How do you answer people who suggest that distance learning is a less valid form of learning?

The vast majority of respondents stated that they had never encountered this attitude. A sample of the submitted responses is presented here.

Answer 1: This is not something that I have encountered but that may be because I am always so positive when I talk about it to people.

Answer 2: I don't think I've encountered any real cynicism about online and distance learning. However, I have seen a number of puzzled looks.

Answer 3: Oddly, my experience has been the opposite. I was in a discussion recently with a professor at a local university, who complained about overcrowded courses, international students as university "cash cows", students cheating and buying degrees, and the difficulty of awarding poor grades or administering discipline. When I described my course, she was genuinely amazed, and wanted to know more about it.

Answer 4: I think the subject matter may contribute to that perception. They don't see my study as contributing toward a practical goal, like taking an accounting course. (Although I was an English major and encountered that same attitude: "What are you going to do with your degree? Do you want to teach?" Every. Single. Time.)

Answer 5: Based on my own experience, 15 or 20 years ago, some people regarded online learning as a less valid form of learning. I had an undergraduate professor say to me once, "Don't ever do an online degree. People will think that you didn't earn it, you just bought it." Times have definitely changed. Today online learning is very much accepted by employers, professors, students, etc. It opens up opportunities for people, who otherwise might not have access. I've noticed a trend recently with blended courses, those that have both an in-person component as well as an online one. I suppose it's been a natural progression from the correspondence courses of yesteryear to where we are today. In terms of this particular course, I've only had people react positively when I mention that I am doing it.

Answer 6: I guess it firstly depends on the personal background: people who experienced and valued their own academic face-to-face career may still see online studies as a lesser value thing, while others who never went to university may see in it an outstanding personal education effort. And secondly, it depends on education culture: Here in XXXXX, distance learning used to be associated with personal limits and is now increasingly associated with overcoming them.

Question 3: I am seeking your views on what, for want of a better word, I am going to call "branding" (if anyone can suggest a better word I would be grateful). By this I mean the elements – principally the use of icons, colour schemes, PowerPoint templates, music in videos etc – that make our programmes look "pulled together" and instantly recognisable to students when they log on. Does this matter to you?

Answer 1: I believe that including unique elements in order to give a distinctive appearance is an important factor. The use of colour schemes can often grab attention far better than words. When I log into Manchester, I don't need to read the bookmark title as the distinctive purple colour makes it immediately identifiable. The same could be said for the use of icons and, personally, I enjoy seeing the new icon each month on the tutor boards. I think visual stimulation helps in an online environment. Although the use of such things may have little value in a physical classroom, you would be surrounded by other sights to arouse interest. With regards to the music, I must admit I am neither for nor against it. It is nice to have a short intro in order to get pens and notebooks ready and the music is pleasant enough – it has never grabbed my attention though.

Answer 2: I hate the music that introduces the lectures. It was used on training videos in my day job. Bad connotations.

Answer 3: I like the fact that there is a consistent use of icons and colour, at least I know I haven't accidentally been logged into something else! If there were no consistent template, I might think it was a bit amateurish, this is because we associate a 'polished' appearance with quality.

Answer 4: My own view is that the branding is more important than it might at first appear. It's recognisable and a symbol of quality and consistency. It also promotes a sense of belonging.

Answer 5: It is reassuring to have the Manchester branding on-screen. Because I'm sat here on my own and not actually in Manchester with you all, I think that branding helps to make it feel like a unified whole.

Works cited

Alberti, S. J. M. M. (2009). *Nature and Culture: Objects, Disciplines and the Manchester Museum*. Manchester: Manchester University Press.
Bolton, P. (2012). *Education: Historical Statistics*. London: House of Commons.

Cain, S. (2012). *Quiet: The Power of Introverts in a World that can't Stop Talking.* London: Penguin.
Carruthers, W. (2015). Introduction: Thinking About Histories of Egyptology. In W. Carruthers, ed. *Histories of Egyptology: Interdisciplinary Measures.* London: Routledge, 1–15.
Champion, T. (2003). Beyond Egyptology: Egypt in 19th and 20th Century Archaeology and Anthropology. in P. Ucko and T. Champion, eds. *The Wisdom of Egypt: Changing Visions through the Ages.* London: UCL Press, 161–85: 180.
Ennis, C., N. Dixon, K. Loscher, J. O'Carroll and D. Ryan (2017). *Strategies for Enhancing the Mature Student Experience in Higher Education.* Dublin: Dublin Institute of Technology.
Gill, A. (2007). Experiences with Developing an On-line Certificate in Egyptology at the University of Manchester. *Learning and Teaching in Action,* Manchester Metropolitan University 5:1, 23–6.
Janssen, R. M. (1992). *The First Hundred Years: Egyptology at University College London, 1892–1992.* London: University College London.
Kearns, M. A. (2014). Risk Worth Taking? A Study of Mature Students' Experiences in Two Irish Universities. *Journal of Postgraduate Research, Trinity College Dublin,* 92–108.
McVitty, D. and K. Morris (2012). *Never Too Late to Learn: Mature Students in Higher Education.* London: Million+ and the National Union of Students.
Moreno Garcia, J. C. (2015). The Cursed Discipline? The Peculiarities of Egyptology at the Turn of the Twenty-First Century. In W. Carruthers, ed. *Histories of Egyptology: Interdisciplinary Measures.* London: Routledge, 50–63.
National Strategy for Access and Student Success in Higher Education (2014). London: Department for Business, Innovation and Skills.
Simpson, O. (2013). Student Retention in Distance Education: Are We Failing Our Students? *Journal of Open, Distance and e-Learning* 28:2, 105–19.
Stevenson, A. (2015). The Object of Study: Egyptology, Archaeology and Anthropology at Oxford, 1860–1960. In W. Carruthers, ed. *Histories of Egyptology: Interdisciplinary Measures.* London: Routledge, 19–33.
Tyldesley, J. A. (2005). *Egypt: How a Lost Civilization Was Rediscovered.* London: BBC Books.

3 Activities

Sparking student engagement

Joyce Tyldesley

Traditionally, humanities programmes have been taught at universities through a system of formal lectures supported by seminars. In recent years this rigid approach has started to change, with the growing recognition that other teaching techniques (flipped classrooms, hybrid or blended learning etc) can be equally if not more relevant. Nevertheless, in most humanities subjects the face-to-face lecture remains the key component of the teaching strategy. This can cause problems. Timetabling lectures and seminars and matching them to appropriate teaching rooms is a complex and time-consuming operation; students with mobility issues are forced to travel from room to room; student with caring or other responsibilities may be unable to attend lectures scheduled at certain times; all too often, students are unable to enrol for their preferred combination of courses due to timetable clashes. Distance learning, of course, does not need to fit into a faculty-wide timetable; there is no need to schedule teaching times or to scramble to book rooms with appropriate facilities for an online course. Nor, if the course has been properly constructed, will it be affected by the many unforeseeable factors that disrupt face-to-face teaching on a daily basis. Transport delays, a sick tutor, sick students, a previous lecture over-running, public holidays: none of these has a significant effect on online teaching. Unsurprisingly, many university policy makers see this flexibility as one of the prime drivers towards adopting online learning.

Online learning allows a greater flexibility of teaching style. From the outset, Egyptology Online has employed a flipped classroom approach to establish a discussion-based, student-centred teaching and learning model. Formal instruction is provided via weekly learning modules (a combination of lectures, podcasts, vlogs, written texts and recommended readings) rolled out on monthly basis, but the focus of the teaching has always been the asynchronous tutorial group, accessed via a series of discussion boards. The discussion boards provide a good environment for even the most introverted students, enabling the tutor to become a facilitator and moderator as well as an instructor and allowing the teacher–student and student–student interaction which might otherwise be missing from an online course. It has long been recognised that a feeling of community, of being an "insider", promotes effective learning (Wegerif 1998).

Simply put, our teaching method adds a necessary human touch to our online teaching, reducing the distance between staff and students and granting students a "sense of belonging" in their learning environment (Bender 2003: 3). This system, developed through experimentation and feedback rather than theoretical research, refined over the years and varied slightly for the MA programme, remains in place throughout all the Manchester online programmes.

Each year group has, as a minimum:

- A general discussion board open to all students in that year. This is the place for the general discussion of course content plus the wider discussion of Egyptological matters.
- A set of tutorial discussion boards. This is the place for the presentation and discussion of the weekly activity work.
- Additional discussion boards which might be opened as necessary. For example, Certificate Year 3 includes an "Extended Essay Discussion Board", where students are encouraged to talk about their 5,000-word essay.

From the start of Year 1, students are told that all non-private, course-related enquiries addressed to tutors must be posted to the discussion boards, with email communication reserved for private matters (issues of health, finances etc). This ensures that all students benefit from the enquiries and their answers, stops any one student from receiving what is effectively private tuition, and reduces the workload for tutors, who may otherwise be faced with multiple emails asking the same question. For similar reasons, students who live near enough to the university to pop in and ask questions in person are discouraged from doing this.

Students are initially allocated to the tutorial groups on a random basis, with the ideal group holding from 10–15 members. Groups with more than 15 members have a tendency to become repetitive; groups with fewer than 10 members may have limited levels of discussion. Within the tutorial group, it is then possible to create sub-groups of four or five students for group work, as required. As the tutor starts to recognise their learning style, students are reallocated to groups on the basis of their posting frequency, with rapid responders and frequent posters being grouped together and slower and less frequent posters being grouped together. This avoids the tension and loss of engagement that can occur when a board of slower posters is

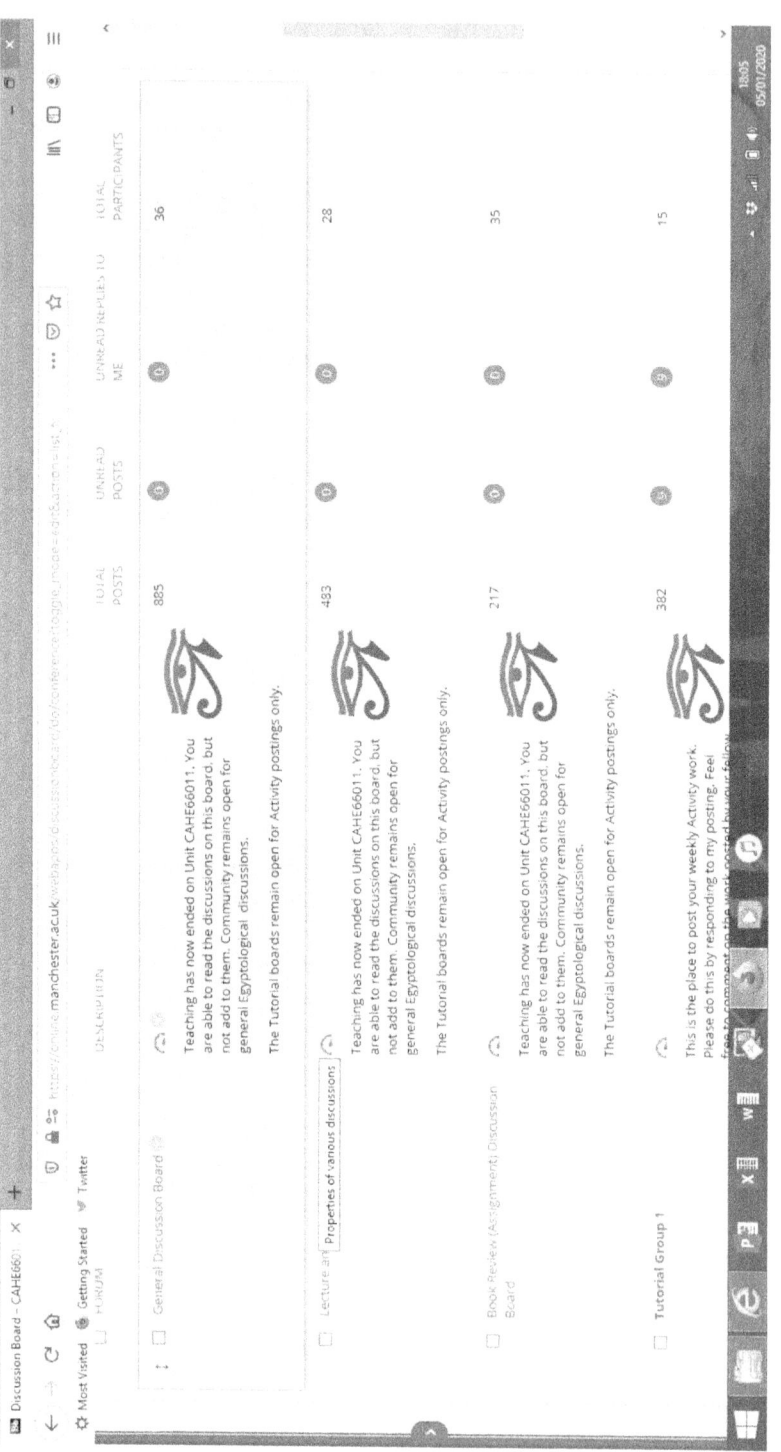

Figure 3.1 A selection of MA discussion boards, showing closed and open boards

faced with a rapid responder, who may be unfairly perceived as attempting to dominate the boards and squash discussion. At the other end of the scale, it avoids the irritation which can occur when a board of rapid responders perceives a slower-posting student as not making a contribution to group work. It needs to be stressed to the students – who often ask how the groups have been allocated – that this is not a value judgement. The fast/frequent posters are not "better" students than the slow/less frequent posters, and the slow/less frequent posters are not being disadvantaged by being excluded from their discussion.

Students are able to edit their posts and, if no one has responded to the thread, to delete them. This edit function is under constant review. It is provided to allow staff or students who make a posting and then immediately notice a spelling mistake or factual error to correct it. We can all sympathise with this situation: sometimes errors mysteriously "appear" as soon as work is published. It is not intended that students should return to posts made several days previously and substantially edit them. This changes the history of the thread and can make responses to the original post look foolish.

Currently, it is possible to hide non-relevant tutorial discussion groups from students in other groups, so that a student in Tutorial Group 1, for example, will only see the general discussion board plus the specific Tutorial Group 1 discussion board. Only the tutor can see all the groups. However, for a brief period following a Blackboard upgrade, students were also able to see all the tutorial group boards, so that the Tutorial Group 1 student could also see, but not access, Tutorial Group 2 and Tutorial Group 3. Crucially, all students were able to see how many postings had been made in all tutorial boards. It was now obvious to everyone that the fast/frequent posting groups had up to three times more postings than the slower and less frequent groups. Instantly, this sparked complaints from the slower groups who had previously been entirely content with their tutorial work. Having seen the figures, they felt that they were missing out on valuable discussion and tuition. This was not the case. The fast/frequent posters were certainly posting more, but their posts were not necessarily of higher quality, with many of the additional posts being polite but essentially meaningless "thank yous" in response to posts made by fellow students. Slower and less frequent posters are less prone to post a simple "thank you". The solution was to a large extent in their own hands; if they too posted more, their figures would rise. But to counter any feeling of unfairness, an open archive was developed. Tutorial discussion board are now locked at the end of each month and transferred to an archive where students in all groups can read the discussion but not make additional postings. New tutorial discussion boards are then opened to process the next month's activity work.

Netiquette

In order to allow discussion to flourish in an environment that is safe and comfortable for all, students are provided with posting guidelines and rules. These attempt to address the fact that students from different cultures will have different ideas of acceptable online behaviour:

- Always be respectful to your fellow students and to your tutors. Any posting that is considered offensive or inappropriate will be deleted by the course tutor. If you feel that someone has made an inappropriate posting, please notify your course tutor.
- Do not use slang, abbreviations, internet abbreviations or sarcasm, as these can be difficult for everyone to understand. Remember, many of our students do not have English as their first language.
- Different nationalities use email and discussion boards in different ways, with some traditionally using long and elaborate introductions, others going straight to the point without a formal greeting. Do not assume that someone is being deliberately rude if they post in a different way to you.
- Every discussion board posting should be of interest to all students on that board. Personal discussions should be conducted by email, rather than on the shared discussion board.
- It is acceptable to post about your holidays, illnesses, pets etc – but these general posting should go to the Community board. The teaching boards are primarily Egyptological in content. Do not worry about this – you will soon understand what is, or what is not, a meaningless or misplaced posting.

Activity work

Each learning module includes a compulsory activity, designed to:

- reinforce active and interactive learning,
- motivate and engage individual learners,
- encourage independent learning,
- encourage group learning,
- share experiences,
- enhance pleasure in learning and
- encourage communication and a sense of community between learners and teachers.

From the teacher's viewpoint, activity work allows tutors to recognise individual student "voices", to monitor student progress and to confirm participation in the programme. Students are instructed that their activity work should be completed and filed in a Personal Portfolio (the student's personal record of progress through the programme, which includes lecture notes, book reviews, reading lists etc) and a summary posted as a response to a tutor-created thread on the tutorial discussion board. Students are encouraged to respond (politely) to the postings made by their fellow students. Students who fail to post their activity work are asked to submit their Personal Portfolio at the end of the academic year as evidence of engagement with (rather than simply logging into) their programme.

The experience of running occasional online Egyptology units for students registered on University of Manchester face-to-face programmes has shown that while courses with a high percentage of mature students will naturally develop lively discussion boards, courses with a high percentage of younger students may not. Face-to-face colleagues report exactly the same situation in tutorials and seminars: younger students will sit and listen but resolutely refuse to speak, while mature students are happy to enter into discussion with the tutor. This parallel situation indicates that although it is possible that the silent posters are not engaged with the subject, or are lazy or are struggling with the activity work, it is far more likely that they simply lack the confidence to speak out in front of their tutor and peers. It may even be that they have lost the habit of contributing to discussion and have become passive learners. On blended courses, it may be that these students are prioritising attendance at lectures, seminars and tutorials over attendance on the online component because their absence from face-to-face units would be immediately obvious to their tutors. In this situation, there are several possible courses of action, which may be combined to create a solution:

- The tutor should from the outset explain in detail the principles underpinning effective e-learning in general and discussion board-based active learning in particular. Students need to be aware that they must participate in discussions, and they also need to know why they should do this.
- One or more icebreakers may be helpful in establishing a community spirit, aiding group bonding and reassuring students that the discussion board is a safe space, free from judgement, abuse and ridicule. The tutor should both complete the icebreaker and respond to each individual student posting.
- The running of the discussion boards could be handed over to the students, with nominated students being responsible for each week's work and the tutor summarising the work at the end of the week. While this may not ensure that every student posts every week, it will ensure that every student posts occasionally.

- An element of compulsion could be introduced, with valid postings to the boards (not simply "I agree with X") contributing towards the final course grade. This element of compulsion forces the first post; subsequent posts then become easier.

Activity work is formative work – it is therefore ungraded. It is designed to encourage cooperation and collaboration rather than competition. However, postings do attract feedback from tutors and fellow students. The first (2004) iteration of the online Certificate was quite clear about the role of the tutor on the discussion board (Gill 2007: 26):

> Whilst tutors were allocated to moderate each discussion group, they were encouraged to intervene only when a discussion needed moving on or clarification, allowing students the opportunity to contribute fully and develop their ideas. . . .
>
> As the tutors changed the groups they facilitated every few months, all students were given the opportunity to benefit from the academics' various areas of expertise.

In the 2007 version of the Certificate, this philosophy was reversed. Tutors are now expected to maintain a very obvious presence on the boards, encouraging students in their work, contributing opinions and opening up new areas of discussion as necessary. It is not always necessary to reply to every posting – this can have the negative effect of halting a developing student-led discussion – but all students at the start of their course appreciate a response. If nothing else, it assures them that they have mastered the posting technology. As familiarity and consistency of teaching staff are an important factor in student satisfaction and learning, so tutors (we have only two plus one part-time linguist; the 2004 course had at least ten) rarely move from group to group in any academic year.

Most activities take one of six basic forms:

- Discuss: students are asked to comment on an aspect of the week's work.
- Read and discuss: students are provided with a set reading (accessible online). They are asked to read, make notes, and answer a set question.
- Watch and discuss: students are provided with a lecture, either specially recorded for the course or in the public domain. They are asked to watch, make notes, and answer a set question.
- Show and tell: students are encouraged to explore online or brick-and-mortar museum resources, finding a specified artefact and sharing it with their fellow students.

- Hieroglyphic translation work-sheet (Certificate, Diploma and Short Courses only).
- Multiple choice quiz (Certificate, Diploma and Short Courses only).

Other, more individual activities may require students perform a specific task. For example:

- Draw a piece of Egyptian art conforming to the ancient Egyptian rules and guidelines.
- Create an ancient Egyptian menu.
- "Excavate" a kitchen cupboard, analysing the contents as if seen by an archaeologist from another culture.
- Draw a map or a family tree.
- Write an ancient Egyptian poem.

All these activities ask well-defined "open" questions intended to promote group discussion: for example, "Why do you think that Khufu built his Great Pyramid?" Closed questions, with an obvious right or wrong, yes or no response – "Where is Khufu's Great Pyramid situated?" are dead ends which do not promote discussion and are avoided. Vague questions ("How do you think the pyramids were built?") may attract no student response simply because the students have no idea how to address this thesis-sized question in the prescribed 250 words. It is important to ensure that activities are evenly "weighted" – they should take the same amount of time to complete and post – although, inevitably, individual students will engage with some activities more than others.

Other forms of activity, including "live" discussions, jigsaw puzzles, word-searches, and crosswords, have been tried but quickly abandoned due to adverse student feedback and, in the case of the jigsaw puzzles etc. technical difficulties encountered by both staff and students. Although e-learning technologists tend to be very keen on the idea of games as teaching aids, our students are fiercely resistant, perceiving these as attempts to "dumb down" Egyptology and to treat students as children. It may be that this is a reflection of both the unusually high age of our students and the low production values of our experimental activities, and that younger students would be more receptive to a well-crafted game; it is clear, however, that if games are to play a part in our learning process, they will have to be appropriately sophisticated.

From the tutor's viewpoint, it is interesting to see how much influence the first poster can wield over the group discussion. Over the past five years, the same article has been set for our Diploma Year 2 students to read and review. In every year, the views of the first student to post have been accepted by the group, even though from year to year the views of the first poster have varied wildly. A tutor posting his/her opinion before all students have had the opportunity to respond to the activity can have the same effect. It is therefore important that any tutor response guides and encourages group discussion, introducing new concepts without expressing too firm a personal opinion. An exception to this rule occurs when a student has posted something that is factually incorrect: mistakes need to be corrected in a tactful and positive way, ideally before they are spotted and corrected by a fellow student, who may be less tactful. Online criticism is visible to all and, being devoid of the vocal inflections and facial expressions which would be obvious in a face-to-face teaching environment, can be perceived as far harsher than intended (Bender 2003: 64).

Activities are primarily designed to be posted straight to the discussion board, with students writing in a friendly, informal style as if talking to the group. Although they should be primarily evidence-based, they do not need formal referencing. However, there is scope for different presentation methods matched to different learning styles, so that a visual learner, for example, might choose to submit a diagram or a graph rather than write a paragraph. Historically, many of our students have encountered technical difficulties when trying to upload images and worksheets to the discussion boards. These difficulties may be the result of outdated computer equipment or of perceived or actual inadequate technical ability, or a combination of the two: failure to participate in an activity then generates both stress and frustration. Activities are therefore designed to avoid these pitfalls. The focus is always on the Egyptological learning objectives and not on developing student computer skills, although as students pass through our programmes they are gradually introduced to new ways of working. We would not, for example, ask Certificate students to create a poster about ancient Egypt as an activity, as this would be challenging, and therefore discouraging, to many. We would, however, ask Master's students to create a poster as part of a graded assignment. As students now have access to increasingly sophisticated computer and photographic equipment (including smart phones), activity styles are reviewed and adjusted on an annual basis. We are now comfortable, for example, asking students to handwrite hieroglyphs and upload them to the boards with the expectation that most, if not all, will be able to comply by uploading a photograph. In 2004, when the Certificate first went online, this would have been impossible, as few students had access to a scanner. Similarly, we have to remember that students have different access to resources (including libraries and museums). We have to make it clear that a "visit" to a museum to look at the Egyptian gallery can be a virtual visit to an online museum.

Activities are compulsory and must be completed before the tutorial discussion board is locked (i.e. within a month of being set). Work completed after the board has been locked should be retained in the Personal Portfolio but cannot be shared on a tutorial board. This cut-off is necessary to allow the course to progress and to encourage the slowest posters – those who always post just a few hours before the board closes – to actually commit to parting with their work. It is important that each activity specifies a minimum and maximum word length to deter both the one-sentence posters and the poster who writes a mini-dissertation on each activity. Observation has shown that it is the excessively lengthy posters who are most resented by their tutorial group colleagues: these posters are perceived as effectively providing a "spoiler" for fellow group members, and their work tends to be ignored by the group. Similarly, students who post their work in the form of an attachment rather than writing on the discussion board, tend to be ignored by fellow students, who are often reluctant to download an attachment from an unknown source.

Far from being resented, this inflexible implementation of due dates and word lengths on an asynchronous course is welcomed by the students, as evidenced by feedback. For example (2019):

> Due to health issues from childhood, the academic path into Egyptology was not accessible to me in the past. Despite my interest in ancient Egypt from a very young age, I had, until now, resigned myself to believing my passion could be nothing more than a private hobby so I was so very grateful when a new avenue was offered. The advantages are numerous i.e. being able to fit study around work, accessing and replaying lectures when needed and chatting with like minded people but being able to withdraw a little if needed. A possible disadvantage I had to take into consideration was the need to be very disciplined when learning outside of a classroom environment. However, I was pleasantly surprised with the course structure, giving monthly deadlines etc. keeps me focused. I researched Egyptology courses purely online – I found a few certificate courses however, they offered fairly unrecognized equivalent university points; they delivered the entire course in one go (it was up to the student to stay motivated and progress); and were taught by a tutor who was only guaranteed to have completed the same course but who would not have necessarily developed further in the field. Manchester offered a solution to every issue – a university accredited course which provided structured learning and was led by known experts in the field. I felt reassured that this course would offer me the best learning experience

Community

"Community" is an online resource outside the teaching boards shared by students in all years on all credit-bearing programmes. It is comprised of a home page housing general information (reading and referencing, study skills, Egyptological resources) plus a series of discussion boards which vary from year to year according to student requirements but which currently include:

- General Forum
- About Me
- Egyptian Events and Media
- Manchester Egyptology Journal Club
- *The Crook and Flail*
- Student Representative Area

Envisaged as the online equivalent of a face-to-face student common room, these discussion boards allow students to discuss anything and everything about ancient Egypt, to post book and film reviews, to introduce themselves to their fellow students, and to relax in *The Crook and Flail*, the Egyptology Online virtual pub. Initially, when Community was launched in 2007, it attracted many daily postings and housed many interesting discussions. It was not unusual for students to visit on Christmas day to spend some quiet time with their fellow students. With the development of social media and, in particular, Facebook groups dedicated to Egyptology, this use has dwindled slightly, but Community still attracts many daily posts.

Unlike the teaching boards, the Community discussion boards are student-led, with the vast majority of the postings expressing individual student opinions. They do not necessarily reflect the views and knowledge of the teaching staff. So students are advised that, as with anything Egyptological, they should read the information with discretion and common sense. Community discussion board threads are archived or deleted either when they become out of date (notifications of lectures which have already happened, television programmes which have already aired, etc.) or when they stop attracting postings.

New students are encouraged to use Community to obtain guidance and reassurance from older students; older students are encouraged to use Community to share their experiences with new students. As Community opens a month before formal teaching starts, it is the place where most students make their first posting to any discussion board. It is suggested – but not compulsory – that all students post a paragraph about themselves, and maybe even a photograph, to the "About Me" board as an icebreaker. For many students this first post is an intimidating and stressful experience; it is therefore important that it occurs in relaxed, non-formal and non-judgemental environment. The expectation is that by the time formal teaching starts, most students have become familiar with the discussion board system, while the tutors have already "met" most of their students.

Our students say

In 2019, our Certificate and Diploma students were asked to comment on their expectations and experiences of isolation and personal connection with both tutors and fellow students while studying on an online programme. Overwhelmingly, the students who responded to this question felt that it was possible to develop a real sense of community amongst online students and staff. A selection of the responses is provided here; again, these have been selected because they raise issues that are likely to be of interest to other online teachers:

> Response 1: I wasn't much troubled by concern that studying online would be a lonely experience. Meeting people face-to-face and having 'live' discussion is, of course, part of the enjoyment of more direct forms of interaction. However, over time, it is possible to form good working relationships with people one only ever meets in a forum. I could be completely wrong about my fellow students on the Diploma but I like to think I have a reasonably rounded impression of them as co-learners, which may be what in the end most matters. I was more concerned about the absence of face-to-face interaction with tutors. Part of this turned out to be wholly misplaced. In my previous courses, we were usually given the choice of several essay titles, and there was also the opportunity to negotiate an individual title with the tutor. I realised that this would not be possible in the way the Manchester course is structured. In the event, however, this has been a great relief. The essay/project titles are so well specified that it is difficult to go wrong. Absence of choice gives greater freedom to pursue the specified line without wasting time. A more general concern about tutor contact was alleviated when any queries I sent by email to the tutor (now tutors) were responded to quickly and warmly. The speed of response may actually be faster and more effective than trying to snatch five minutes with a lecturer in between lectures or at the end of a long evening session.
>
> Response 2: Feeling quite insecure around people, I would have never started any kind of further education after I had (at last!) left school. I do have a higher education degree, but even though this was at a local (technical) university, it did not require to be present in the lectures, and so most of the time I wasn't. I learned for myself and only went there to take the exams or attend the classes that were absolutely necessary. So I didn't make use of the advantages of a "regular" university education anyway, and in the contrary, my low presence brought about some difficulties that I would have avoided

had I been able to behave like a "real" student. On that background, an online-only education was the perfect choice for me, because what I was able to do (write and learn) was actually all that was required. I did not expect any degree of socialising here and was not looking for it – although silently hoping that I might get to know some like-minded people without having them too close to my comfort zone. After three years, I can say that this not only worked, but really helped expanding my comfort zone in an unexpected way. Especially in comparison to those first studies, where the pressure of presence killed any socialising potential for me, this time the low threshold indeed made it possible to choose my pace not only in learning, but even much more in personal contact. I met interesting people all over the world and made close friends where I would have never expect it. My views on the subject obviously expanded hugely, but for me privately, the personal development is a much more important issue, because while it is rather easy for me to gain new knowledge, it is infinitely more difficult to gain and refine social skills and personal contacts.

Response 3: I did a Certificate In Contemporary Science with XXXXX. In 3 years of study I had no contact with either a tutor or other students. I obviously received marks and feedback but there was no exchange or encouragement. It was a very lonely process. I would hate it if some one different every day monitored the boards. I have loved the exchanges we have had and I have made a wonderful group of friends over the years at Manchester which has enriched the study experience.

Response 4: Manchester is my only experience with distance learning, but the personal connection has become quite important to me. I sometimes even refer back to the "About Me" thread when someone outside of my immediate tutorial group posts something interesting and I want to refresh myself on who they are and see them.

Response 5: If you'd asked me before or when first signing up for the course as against now my Responses would have been very different! I've not studied online before and so was fully expecting a rather insular and remote experience, just to be set things to read or think about, get on with it in my own time, and then proffer results sort of thing. I wasn't at all expecting discussions or contacts with other students on the course, and indeed initially welcomed that distance would you believe, as it was so unfamiliar to me. In much the same way, I also expected lecturer 'contact' to be more akin to reading a textbook rather than 'feeling' there was an actual person there. However I am delighted to have found (and been able to ease myself into and fully immerse and enjoy) that this course is nothing like that at all, and in particular that there is a great feeling of confidence and indeed trust in our tutors. It doesn't matter if we don't physically see you or Nicky (either in a recorded lecture or photographs), because we still gain a comfortable rapport and still 'feel' you through course instructions and comments on work and discussions? So I still feel as though I know you through the boards which makes them far more comfortable territory, and also me less likely to worry about posting a question or idea that might seem silly or weak.

Response 6: I certainly want to feel a personal connection with both teachers and students, and I think internet forums are surprisingly effective at generating those connections. I also feel confident that my teachers on this course see enough of me to be able to stretch me in the directions I need stretching. I don't think this would be possible with a frequently rotating staff, as they would not see a sufficient volume of any student's work to identify their overall weak spots and their strengths.

Works cited

Bender, T. (2003). *Discussion-based Online Teaching to Enhance Student Learning: Theory, Practice and Assessment*. Sterling, VA: Stylus Publishing.

Ennis, C., N. Dixon, K. Loscher, J. O'Carroll and D. Ryan (2017). *Strategies for Enhancing the Mature Student Experience in Higher Education*. Dublin: Dublin Institute of Technology.

Gill, A. (2007). Experiences with Developing an On-line Certificate in Egyptology at the University of Manchester. *Learning and Teaching in Action*, Manchester Metropolitan University 5:1, 23–6.

Wegerif, R. (1998). The Social Dimension of Asynchronous Learning Networks. *The Journal of Asynchronous Learning Networks* 2. Available from: www.aln.org/alnweb/journal/vol2_issue!/wegerif.htm

4 Assessment strategies
Problems and solutions
Joyce Tyldesley

All three of the University of Manchester credit-bearing Egyptology programmes (Certificate, Diploma and MA) are assessed by written coursework rather than traditional written examinations. This is a deliberate decision. It is the view of the teaching team that coursework moves assessment away from the simple memorising and regurgitating of facts that occurs when assessing by examination, delegating more responsibility for learning to the student.

Our coursework can take a variety of forms: essays, projects, book reviews, a museum catalogue, a diary etc. The precise requirements for each assessment are explained at the start of each academic year, with students being expected to submit their work on or before a given submission date via a dropbox within the online course. Tutors read the submission and add feedback and a grade. The graded coursework plus feedback are then automatically returned to the students on a specified day. Additional generic feedback is provided on the discussion boards once all coursework has been returned. Students are then encouraged to discuss their essays, ask questions and, if they wish, share their work. They are not, however, encouraged to share their grades. Long experience has shown that grade sharing always makes at least one student, and often two, unhappy.

We have, in the past, experimented with computer-based testing: an examination week when a series of multiple choice and short-answer questions with a set time limit were made available to students. These had to be open-book tests, as it was impossible to prevent students working at home from consulting their notes and equally impossible to require students to attend an assessment centre where they could work under strict examination conditions. The tests caused problems for students unaccustomed to having to log into the course at a set time – some were, for example, unavoidably away from home on business when they should have been online – and caused great stress when internet connections failed. From the tutor's viewpoint, it was necessary to create a huge bank of questions to ensure that no two students received exactly the same test. This was difficult, as humanities subjects are not naturally suited to multiple choice and short answer questions. It had been intended to experiment with more traditional-style online exams – two or three open book essays and a two hour time-limit, for example – but given the problems encountered during the shorter tests, plus the growing realisation that this was not the most appropriate method of examining our students, this was abandoned.

Although we have made the process as simple as possible, comments on the discussion boards make it clear that the writing and submission of a piece of coursework is an intensely stressful situation for many students. It is particularly stressful for those who have been out of education for many years, and who fear that they are now unable to write to an appropriate standard. Non-native English speakers may feel additional pressure, as they worry about completing a long piece of work in a foreign language. Indeed, we would routinely "lose" two or three Certificate students as the first essay deadline approached, some students preferring to drop out of the programme entirely rather than submit what they feared may be a substandard piece of work. In order to reduce the stress levels we:

- Created an assignment handbook that explained in great detail every practical aspect of assignment writing and submission, including titles, submission dates, word lengths, font and page sizes, links to suggested resources, and an explanation of the grading criteria.
- Stressed the importance of making regular posts to the discussion boards as practice for writing a longer piece of written work.
- Provided a comprehensive study-skills section on Community, including information on learning styles, reading, referencing and the use of the university library online resources.
- Discussed the essays on the boards well in advance of their submission date, stressing that these should not be regarded as tests but as learning experiences designed to help each student grow in knowledge and skill.
- Provided a sample essay (with an unrelated title) to show this standard of writing and referencing required.
- Created activities focused on basic essay-writing skills such as referencing and the avoidance of plagiarism.

Blackboard (our virtual platform) allows tutors to see how many students have read the tutor feedback on their graded essays. This is sometimes disappointingly low: although the feedback is designed to boost student confidence and help with future assignment work, it often goes unread. This would suggest that it is the grade (automatically revealed in "My Grades") which causes student stress rather than the feedback, which has to be actively sought out and can be conveniently ignored. We therefore took the decision to allow students to submit a first ungraded assignment under exactly the same conditions as subsequent graded work. Everyone who submitted this first piece of work received a grade of 100% plus detailed feedback. This had the instant effect of halting the pre-submission drop-outs. By the time the next, graded, coursework became due, students felt comfortable with the system, and there was no associated loss of students.

The international student

Our student body is drawn from countries worldwide: in 2013–14, for example, our students came from Australia, Belgium, Bermuda, Brazil, Canada, Croatia, Egypt, Finland, Germany, Greece, Ireland, the Netherlands, Poland, Spain, Sweden, Thailand, the United Kingdom and the United States. This naturally means that our students come from a wide range of educational backgrounds. Tutors need to be aware that this can lead to confusion and disappointment at assessment time. There are three issues that recur from year to year:

Spellings and the meaning of words

As the University of Manchester is a British university, it expects assessed work to be written in English-English. The students who have the most trouble with this requirement are our US students, who are accustomed to using US-English spellings and who may not have previously realised that other English variants exist. This is not a problem on the informal discussion boards, where there are no strict rules of presentation, but it does become a problem (albeit minor) when writing a formal essay. Students are therefore specifically told to check their work using a UK-English spell-check. Even so, there are some students who are surprised when they realise that "color" and "center" are not standard English-English spellings. As an extension of this, there are some words – "rubber", "period" and "thong" come to mind – which have different meanings in different countries, and some symbols or signs which may be obvious to students of one nationality, less so to others. This language barrier is something for teachers to bear in mind when setting assignment submission dates: 10/12/2020 will mean different things to different students, but 10 December 2020 will be obvious to everyone.

Response to grades

Universities in different countries have different grading criteria. Under the British system, a grade of 70+ is a First Class grade. Anyone receiving

70% (14/20) is therefore to be congratulated. In other countries, however, grades are typically much higher, and 70% is not considered a remarkable achievement. We have found it advisable to explain this to students, warning them that they will be expected to accept the British system and providing them with a "conversion" chart indicating UK/rest of world equivalent grades. Even so, almost every year we have a student devastated or angry over a grade that we, in Manchester, regard as excellent. The most extreme example of this led to a student with a 90% grade declining to progress to the next year on the grounds that she was "not good enough".

Poor academic practice

In some educational environments students are not expected to develop a critical approach to their learning. They learn by studying the work of experts and reproducing it. That is not what we expect from our students. We therefore spend time at the start of each year explaining that coursework must be written in the student's own words, and must include citations and references. Despite this, students will occasionally submit work that demonstrates what we consider to be poor academic practice or poor referencing. This may not be deliberate cheating. For example:

- An inexperienced student might fail to reference information obtained from another source without any intent to deceive.
- A student might come from an academic background where an unacknowledged quotation is considered a mark of respect to the original author.
- A student for whom English is a second language may not feel sufficiently confident to write about ancient Egypt in his or her own words.
- A student may include an excessive number of referenced quotations in his or her own work, linking the quotations together with a few original words, so that essentially the essay is written by someone else.

Our students are given activities throughout their programme to help them identify and avoid these pitfalls.

The cheating student

It is often assumed that the online classroom makes life easy for the dishonest student. In fact, the cheating student is an unfortunate feature of all learning environments, online or otherwise. Colleagues who have invigilated written examinations have reported students substituting for other students (complete with borrowed ID and, on more than one occasion, a face-concealing disguise) and students with information written on various surfaces including calculator covers, water bottle labels, limbs and, in one enterprising case, edible rice-paper. Colleagues who have examined written coursework have also detected examples of deliberate, premeditated cheating (plagiarism, collusion and essays purchased from online stores). The ongoing challenge – invigilator versus cheat – is considered such a normal part of academic life that it rarely features in pedagogic discussion: it is seen as something quite separate from teaching. The steps taken to combat plagiarism on our online programmes – student education and the use of an electronic detection system (Turnitin) to screen all submitted work – are exactly the same steps as those taken to combat plagiarism on face-to-face programmes.

Could online students employ substitutes to complete their work on a regular basis? I would be the first to agree that it would entirely possible for registered online student (A) to persuade another person (B) to complete an online course, so that A emerged from the process with a Certificate earned by B. It is doubtful that any university would spot this substitution. It is equally doubtful that any university would spot this level of substitution on a face-to-face programme either. This scheme would, however, require B to act as a substitute student throughout the entire programme; it would almost certainly be far easier for A to simply forge a Certificate!

What about a one-off substitution? A asking B to write just one essay, for example? This is less likely to go undetected on an online course than on a face-to-face course, as online tutors who teach via discussion boards quickly become very familiar with their students' written work. A new author would lead to an obvious change of style and technical ability, and this would ring warning bells. Online courses that do not have a strong degree of staff–student interaction, however, may be vulnerable in this area and may need to take more robust steps to prevent substitution. Similarly, online courses examined by quizzes and short answer questions may have difficulties identifying substitute students.

Quizzes

Monthly multiple-choice quizzes are included in the suite of Certificate and Diploma activities. These are not summative tests but an opportunity for students to test and extend their knowledge. Students are encouraged to complete the test, revise their incorrect responses, and retake the test until they achieve 100%. The tests are automatically graded, with the highest grade being recorded within the programme for the student's information only.

Our students say

Students were asked about the perceived drawbacks to online learning. Several responded by highlighting the problem of the cheating student.

> Response 1: I see that the problem of this type of online course is about the identification of the student. Sorry to raise this question but I also would like to know that how the University know that the essay/projects are really done by those individual students? What if they hire someone else to write the essay/projects for them? Because in face-to-face class, to do an exam, the student must show the ID card to identify themselves before doing an exam but this process is neglected for the online course, so maybe this is one of the reason that peoples think the online course is less-valid form of learning? But in my opinion, normally the students who apply for the online course should be keen to study by themselves and don't cheat.
>
> Response 2: I have never heard the suggestion of online accredited courses being less valid than conventional, classroom learning, but I have heard people comment that online courses makes it easier for the student to cheat – submitted essays being seen as a main area. My answer to this is that essays written on behalf of another can just as easily be done in conventional face-to-face teaching. However, all students have their own style of writing and it is insulting to the tutor to think that they would not recognise something submitted in a totally different style to the student's usual work. If a student wishes to cheat, no matter where or what they are studying they will try to do so.
>
> Response 3: Issues around cheating etc are as valid in online as well as in on-campus.
>
> Response 4: I work in a university and the development of online courses is essential in today's market and as far as I can see, they are subject to the same scrutiny and checks as a more traditional on-campus based course.
>
> Response 5: There are some who think that Distance Learning part time means that the pressure of studying for a full time degree is lessened, and that therefore distance learners have an advantage. If anyone does think that they can have a chat with me about what it is like to study for a degree while working full time, for a bit of context.

5 Lectures and podcasts
Creation and optimal use

Nicky Nielsen

The backbone of the suite of Egyptology distance learning courses at the University of Manchester is the three-pronged teaching strategy centred around passive learning, active learning and independent learning. These three areas are covered respectively by recorded lectures, monitored discussion boards and written assessments. This chapter will firstly explore the role and development of recorded/video lectures within the broader field of distance education and secondly use the technological methodologies employed by the Egyptology Online course creators at the University of Manchester as a case study of a cost-effective and popular lecture creation format. This will include an analysis and discussion of relevant survey data gathered from previous and current students on the various Egyptology courses.

E-lectures and distance education: development, benefits and challenges

While institutions such as the Open University began utilising the medium of television for the purposes of hosting what might loosely be termed lectures for their students (see for instance Bates 1988), a great deal of first-generation online distance learning simply did not employ lectures, visual or auditory, relying rather on the dissemination of written materials to their student cohorts. As argued in 2005 by Keegan:

> For the purpose of helping students with their understanding the almost total absence of lectures in distance teaching need not be a serious loss. It is never to be expected that students will leave a lecture with any significant internalization of the concepts used and described by the lecturer.
>
> (2005: 143)

While the final sentence is most certainly one which is open to argument, Keegan's argument that lectures should not necessarily be considered a required, or even desirable, component of a distance learning course has been echoed by other authors, for instance in the context of the flipped classroom approach (Pierce and Fox 2012). Other research has also shown that, as a rule, creating a lecture for a distance learning cohort takes longer than creating one for a face-to-face cohort (Visser 2000).

The rapid development in communication technology over the past decade has naturally changed the landscape of how lectures can be prepared and delivered to e-learning cohorts. New types of software (such as ONELab, Furini, Galli and Martini 2019) can be employed both to produce higher-quality content and also lessen the work load on course conveners. Other technologies can be employed to address the specific needs of distance learning students with disabilities (see for instance Singhal et al. 2019; Kent et al. 2018).

The increased use of lecture capture technologies in universities both in the United Kingdom and internationally has in some sense reignited the debate surrounding the efficacy of recorded lectures, with some research finding little difference in terms of student knowledge retention and engagement between cohorts either attending face-to-face lectures or relying on recorded lectures (McLean and Suchman 2016), while other research shows a variety of benefits and drawbacks to both models (see for instance Elliott and Neal 2016; Khan 2016; Edwards and Clinton 2019; Karnad 2013; O'Brien and Verma 2019). In a sense, this corpus of research is interesting and helpful to distance learning instructors, but it must be underlined that the results of such research are not always relevant. In the case of courses which are 100% distance learning, course tutors do not have a genuine choice between allowing students to attend physical lectures or rely on lecture recordings, as there are no physical lectures held as part of the course.

Rather than rely on research related to the benefits and drawbacks which can be drawn by face-to-face cohorts from lecture capture, distance learning instructors should instead look to the corpus of excellent research on the same topic with regards to distance education and e-learning cohorts. Ronchetti (2010: 45) identified four main benefits to the integration of pre-recorded lectures within the context of a distance learning course:

> a) help working-students by bridging the gap given by their absence during regular lectures; b) support regular students by giving them the opportunity to recover lectures lost due to forced or elective absence; c) assist students having difficulties with the lecture's spoken language; d) give students a means to review critical sections and check their notes.

To these can be added what may sound as a somewhat more ethereal concept but one which is nevertheless crucial to student retention and student satisfaction: a sense of belonging to a community of learners.

Potential drawbacks to using exclusively e-lectures to teach online is obvious: it promotes an overreliance on knowledge transmission and does not foster the engagement and independent thinking which are the hallmarks of higher education. As such, recorded lectures or e-lectures should never be used by themselves as an educational tool but paired with – for instance – discussion activities or other interactive tools which can serve in place of face-to-face seminars, which to a greater extent prioritise student engagement and knowledge exchange, as opposed to the unidirectional knowledge transmission provided by lectures in face-to-face teaching. Another, more practical issue is that creating lectures for distance learning cohorts represent a greater investment in terms of time and resources than the equivalent for a face-to-face cohort (Visser 2000, see also Olson and McCracken 2015).

Before progressing to the specific case study of lecture development within the Egyptology Online courses at the University of Manchester, it is important to briefly touch upon the issue of synchronous versus asynchronous lectures. While some authors such as Skylar (2009) have concluded that students will – if given the choice – favour the more interactive synchronous modes of teaching (with, for instance, live-streaming lectures) to the asynchronous pre-recorded lectures, this debate misses a crucial and immovable obstacle: time zones.

On any course with a large and diverse international cohort it is impossible to identify a specific time when both course instructors and all students in all time zones can be available. As such, some students will always be disadvantaged based on their geographical location. For instance, if a course is taught in the United Kingdom (GMT), students in Australia and the United States are most likely to be unavailable to participate in synchronous activities, whereas students based elsewhere in Europe or the Middle East might in some circumstances be better placed to take part. The issue of students across different time zones can be addressed through a complex system of scheduling (hosting, for instance, multiple live sessions during a day to maximise the chance of students from all time zones finding a time convenient to them), but this method presents problems in terms of scheduling for both students and tutors (Hovenga 1999). This option arguably also requires a more flexible and larger teaching staff and as such is not necessarily applicable across all learning institutions. Alternatively, the live-streaming can be recorded and so viewed later by students who cannot participate in the synchronous event itself (see for instance a discussion of this method in Van Zyl and Powell 2012). However, this creates an unnecessary and potential harmful distinction between students based on their geographical origin and can foster a sense among some students that they are denied opportunities for learning simply based on their national/geographic origin or current abode.

Egyptology e-lectures at the University of Manchester

While Egyptology at the University of Manchester was originally taught as a face-to-face evening class and then as a correspondent's course, it moved to an online platform in September 2004. Initially, lectures were not utilised on the course, nor were they requested by students, many of whom did not have access to private computers or, if they had, did not have access to internet connections of a sufficient speed to support streaming video. The teaching material, in the form of journal articles, high-resolution images and original written content, was uploaded to the University of Manchester's Virtual Learning Environment, which at the time was hosted on WebCT. This platform also allowed for the creation and maintenance of monitored discussion boards which provided the primary conduit of tutor-student engagement. The course ran for four years without any e-lectures until 2008 when discussions concerning the incorporation of a smaller number or experimental e-lectures were conducted.

The first e-lectures taught on the suite of online Egyptology courses (Figure 5.1) were synchronous in nature. Recorded using Wimba and hosted on the WebCT platform, the format allowed students to view the lecturer's PowerPoint slides on the left-hand side of the screen, while the right-hand side was divided into an upper and lower quadrant. In the upper, the lecturer was visible through a live video feed, while the lower quadrant hosted a chat box allowing students to type comments in real time. These comments allowed the lecturer to respond to queries and questions in real time. While on the surface a very useful and interactive format, the rapid expansion of the student cohort to include larger numbers of international students soon meant that the course catered to students based in as many as eight different time zones. This meant that some students, those who had work or personal commitments, and those based, for instance, in the United States or Australia could not easily find the time to attend lectures which were hosted during the day in Manchester (GMT). This meant that either the students had to rearrange their work and care responsibilities, thereby removing one of the major benefits of the distance learning model, namely its flexibility, or alternatively had to view the lectures as recordings which were uploaded immediately following the end of the live-stream. This resulted in a high number of student complaints, as students based in the most distant time zones felt relegated to second-tier status by comparison to their colleagues in Europe.

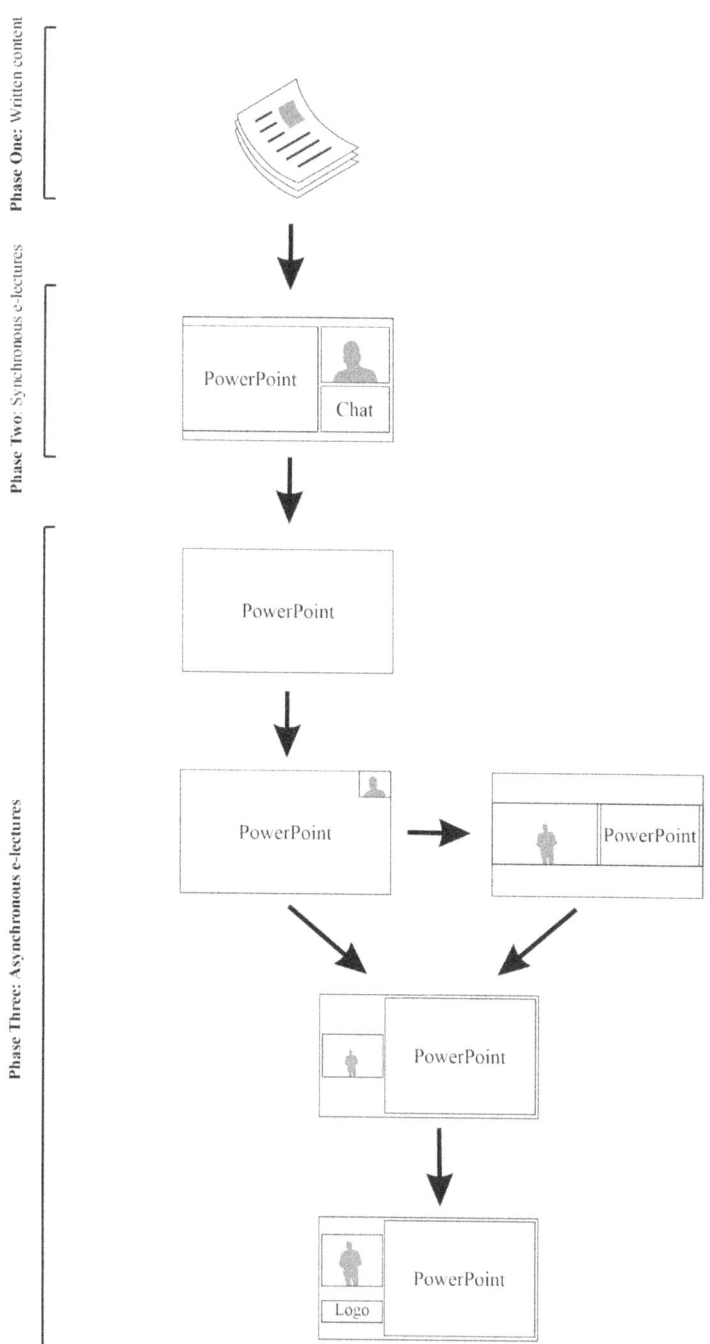

Figure 5.1 Schematic Overview: The development of lecturing technologies utilised on the Manchester Egyptology Online programmes from 2004 to the current day

Experimental attempts to engage students via live video feeds were also attempted. Students were encouraged to use webcams and microphones to communicate with each other and tutors, but not all students had access to the relevant hardware. As a result, funding was sought to purchase webcams and headsets, which were then mailed to the students, but in many cases packages were lost or misdirected, causing further confusion and complaints.

As a direct result of these complaints, the synchronous lecture model was discontinued in 2008 with the move of the courses from WebCT to the Blackboard platform. In its place, the lectures became simpler, consisting of a full-screen PowerPoint synchronised to an audio-only lecture. While more popular than the synchronous lectures, this format was criticised by the student body for being too impersonal. While some research (e.g. Berner and Adams 2004) has argued that there is little difference between visual and audio lectures in terms of student satisfaction and learning, this was certainly not reflected in terms of the University of Manchester cohort. The Manchester students felt strongly that seeing the lecturer was important for them to feel part of the course and part of a distance learning community. In response to this, a small video-box was added in a corner of the PowerPoint showing the lecturer during the recording. This system worked well, although it required access to a soundproof booth and professional-grade recording equipment. The lectures were recorded by the lecturer seated in the sound booth in front of a webcam.

In 2017, increased pressures on university resources and increased difficulties in gaining access to the sound booth prompted a re-evaluation of this recording strategy. Through consultations with university e-learning and media services departments, it was decided that a pilot study focused around utilising the university's newly installed video capture system should be launched. The use of this system would allow the lecturer to record lectures in a lecture theatre, a more natural environment for many academics. As the video capture system employs tracking cameras, this method would also give lecturers more flexibility and movability, allowing a more spontaneous and natural style of delivery.

The first step of the process was two test recordings in April 2018 aimed at identifying potential quality issues (such as low audio and poor video quality) and technological issues (such as issues with uploading/editing videos and booking recordings). These tests were then followed by 12 hours (over three days) of lecture recordings for the three Short Courses in Speech of the Gods: Introduction to Middle Egyptian Hieroglyphs. Despite some initial issues surrounding the process of editing and downloading the raw footage, the lectures were successfully recorded and incorporated into the Short Course. Following this successful proof of concept, a strategy meeting was held between Egyptology staff wherein the possibility of expanding the use of the technology to all future Egyptology Online lectures was discussed. To ensure student input, a trial lecture was recorded and uploaded on a separate discussion board (available to all registered Egyptology students) together with one of the old-style lectures recorded seated in a sound booth. The students were encouraged to watch both lectures and were provided with a link to an anonymous survey. They were also given access to an anonymised discussion board and encouraged to state which lecture delivery mode they preferred. The results of the survey showed a clear preference for the new lectures (53% of the students were in favour of the new mode, 13% in favour of the old and 34% had no preference either way), with the anonymous discussion board producing similar results. Many of the students commented on the feeling of inclusion that the new mode of delivery gave them. In the words of one:

> The key point about the new format is that it is more engaging. This is not to do with the quality of the speaker or the nature of the material but simple the speaker is more animated and natural. Also, the new format enables me, as a distance student, for more "on campus" more of a sense that I can "go to a lecture". So, it allows me to feel more connected to the course.

The primary criticism of the new mode of lecture delivery was the ratio between the half of the screen showing the lecturer standing in front of the classroom and the synchronised PowerPoint. Due to the video rendering software used by the university, the PowerPoint became relatively small and text-heavy slides were difficult to read. After further consultation with media services, this was remedied by downloading, cutting and re-splicing the two feeds together using the video editing software Filmora9 to present the lectures in the final format shown in Figure 5.1, which shrinks the portion of the screen taken up by the lecturer in order to enlarge the section of the screen carrying the PowerPoint. As a final stage, a stationary digital camera was utilised to shoot the feed of the lecturer in the room in place of the lecture capture cameras. A separate screen capture software was used to record the PowerPoint, as well as the audio from a stationary podcast microphone plugged in to the laptop. This final setup provides both high definition video and clear audio and so has become the preferred format.

Through the years, the format and layout of these e-lectures has developed with the appearance and availability of new technologies, and more importantly as a direct response to student feedback. During the years of teaching distance learning, the importance of relying on and listening to student feedback – not just through the standardised university feedback procedures but also through anonymous discussion boards and surveys – when new technologies or changes to the course structures are proposed has proven invaluable in guiding the course conveners and university e-learning departments.

Incorporating podcasts and vlogs: student survey results and analysis

The definition of a podcast in this context is an audio-only file which is made available to the students through Blackboard and which – as opposed to a lecture, which usually revolves around a single tutor – brings together a group of two or more experts for a more informal discussion of a topic or concept. Recent research (cf Nielsen, Andersen and Dau 2018) has highlighted the usefulness of podcasts both in online learning and in blended classrooms, along with the more practical benefits from the point of view of university management and course tutors, namely that podcasts are:

> cheap to produce, requiring little more than simple recording software and a microphone. They are also easy to distribute thanks to sites like iTunes and Podbay, making radio-style broadcast possible for educators around the world. It is little wonder, then, that podcast usage in education institutions has steadily grown since the emergence of the medium in the early 2000s.
>
> (Drew 2017: 49)

Egyptology at Manchester utilises a Rode RØDE NT-USB microphone connected to an HP computer, with the recordings done on the in-built Microsoft recording software 'Sound Recorder' and edited with Filmora9. While the Manchester podcasts are not yet hosted on iTunes, but for security purposes are hosted on the internal Blackboard server to ensure that they are not downloaded and shared by students, they nevertheless function in a similar manner to those hosted by external sites such as iTunes and Soundcloud.

Their value within the context of the Manchester Egyptology courses is that podcasts add an element of non-structured discourse between subject specialists, providing a more informal and friendly atmosphere for students to learn. Post-production editing is kept deliberately minimal, leaving side discussions, digressions and jokes between tutors within the recording. The format broadly follows an interview style, with one designated tutor taking the lead and directing the discussion, ensuring that predetermined topics and points are covered. In advance of a recording, participants are provided with a prompt sheet containing specific facts about the topic under discussion which should be mentioned along with a list of general themes. Another method is based around a quote from a specific source which is read in full by the lead tutor/"interviewer" at the beginning of the podcast and which then becomes the focal point of the discussion.

An example of this is a postgraduate level podcast episode titled The Overlooked Egyptologists which focuses on the Eurocentric tendencies of Egyptology to overlook or ignore native Egyptian archaeologists and their contributions to the development of the field. This episode is opened with a one-paragraph quote from the book *Labels: A Mediterranean Journal* by the British author Evelyn Waugh, wherein Waugh criticises the Egyptians for never having produced, in his opinion, a well-trained Egyptologist. The discussion then centres around the validity of Waugh's opinion and the colonial context of his statement and attitudes.

Another benefit of the podcast as a method of expert-led communication and teaching is that guest lecturers can more easily be brought onto the course to contribute on their specialisms. The podcast does not require the booking of rooms but, as previously mentioned, only requires a quiet room and recording equipment, ideally in the form of a side-address microphone of sufficient quality to ensure that students receive a high-quality product.

Prior to the introduction of podcasts to the full range of online courses in Egyptology at the University of Manchester a podcast was recorded by two tutors and uploaded to a specially created discussion board. Students were encouraged to listen to the podcast and post their thoughts either with their names or anonymously. It was explained clearly that the podcasts were not envisaged as a replacement for lectures but rather an addition to lectures, discussion boards, readings and other course materials. The student feedback was overwhelmingly positive, with the students broadly falling into two groups. The first was those who had regular experience of using podcasts and who welcomed something they felt was familiar and known onto the course ("I am a great fan of podcasts as a way of giving information in a more informal way") – but who also asked for the podcasts to be uploaded to external hosting sites, to make them easier to copy onto MP3 players and smartphones ("One thing I'd add to the suggestions that have already been made is to make sure people can download it to listen to offline") and the second was students who had never listened to podcasts before ("This was my first ever podcast").

As a final development, staff have experimented with using short vlogs ("video logs") to communicate with the students. Instead of a written message uploaded to Blackboard or sent via group email, a circa 1-minute vlog is recorded with the aid of a simple webcam setup in a staff office. This video is then uploaded to Blackboard. Preliminary feedback from students suggests that this helps to breakdown the perceived digital barrier between tutor and student by helping the students put a face to a wider range of the lecturers who teach them. In combination with recorded lectures and podcasts, the vlogs can help provide a more positive working relationship between tutors and their cohort, thereby helping student retention and classroom cohesion.

Conclusion

The usefulness of e-lectures has remained a point of debate, a debate which will undoubtedly continue with each new technology incorporated into the rapidly growing industry of distance education. However, e-lectures – along with physical lectures for face-to-face students – nevertheless remain a valid and useful tool for the transmission of knowledge from a tutor to a cohort. Overreliance on lectures to the exclusion of more interactive and student-led discussion activities can however be detrimental to student satisfaction and retention, to the same extent as an exclusive reliance on, for instance, written materials with no interactive, video or audio content can. Distance learning is in the end about balancing the different types of teaching strategies and methodologies to create a coherent whole which both provides equal value to students as a face-to-face course and also allows distance learning students to feel like parts of a dedicated learning community.

Podcasts both within distance, blended and face-to-face learning represent a different way of communicating expertise, one which does not need to be as constrained by unidirectional formality as a traditional lecture, and crucially one which can be teacher created with very limited resources and technological expertise. This ease should however in no way be used as an argument to suggest that podcasts can in any significant capacity replace more formal learning technologies like e-lectures or discussion groups but should rather be viewed as a useful addition, one which allows students to get to know their tutors in a more informal setting and in this way contribute to their sense of community and belonging.

Works cited

Alexander, S. and D. Boud (2001). Learners Still Learn from Experience When Online. In J. Stephenson, ed. *Teaching & Learning Online: New Pedagogies for New Technologies*. Routledge: Oxford.
Bates, A. W. (1988). Television, Learning and Distance Education. *Journal of Educational Television* 14:3, 213–25.
Berner, E.S. and B. Adams (2004). Added value of video compared to audio lectures for distance learning. *International Journal of Medical Informatics* 73:2, 189–193.
Drew, C. (2017). Edutaining Audio: An Exploration of Education Podcast Design Possibilities. *Educational Media International* 54:1, 48–62.

Edwards, M. R. and M. E. Clinton (2019). A Study Exploring the Impact of Lecture Capture Availability and Lecture Capture Usage on Student Attendance and Attainment. *Higher Education* 77:3, 403–21.

Elliott, C. and D. Neal (2016). Evaluating the Use of Lecture Capture Using a Revealed Preference Approach. *Active Learning in Higher Education* 17:2, 153–67.

Furini, M., G. Galli and M. C. Martini (2019). An Online Education System to Produce and Distribute Video Lectures. *Mobile Networks and Applications*, 1–8

Hovenga, E. J. (1999). Using Multi-media to Enhance a Flexible Learning Program: Lessons Learned. *Proceedings of the AMIA Symposium 1999*, 530–4.

Karnad, A. (2013). *Student Use of Recorded Lectures: A Report Reviewing Recent Research into the Use of Lecture Capture Technology in Higher Education, and Its Impact on Teaching Methods and Attendance*. LSE Report, London.

Keegan, D. (2005). *Theoretical Principles of Distance Education*. Routledge: Oxford.

Kent, M., K. Ellis, N. Latter and G. Peaty (2018). The Case for Captioned Lectures in Australian Higher Education. *TechTrends* 62:2, 158–65.

Khan, H. U. (2016). Possible Effect of Video Lecture Capture Technology on the Cognitive Empowerment of Higher Education Students: A Case Study of Gulf-based University. *International Journal of Innovation and Learning* 20:1, 68–84.

McLean, J. L. and E. L. Suchman (2016). Video Lecture Capture Technology Helps Students Study Without Affecting Attendance in Large Microbiology Lecture Courses. *Journal of Microbiology & Biology Education* 17:3, 480.

Nielsen, S. N., R. H. Andersen and S. Dau (2018). Podcast as a Learning Media in Higher Education. In *ECEL 2018 17th European Conference on e-Learning*. Academic Conferences and Publishing Limited, 424–30.

O'Brien, M. and R. Verma (2019). How Do First Year Students Utilize Different Lecture Resources? *Higher Education* 77:1, 155–72.

Olson, J. S. and F. E. McCracken (2015). Is It Worth the Effort? The Impact of Incorporating Synchronous Lectures into an Online Course. *Online Learning* 19:2.

Pierce, R. and J. Fox (2012). Vodcasts and Active-learning Exercises in a 'Flipped Classroom' Model of a Renal Pharmacotherapy Module. *American Journal of Pharmaceutical Education* 76:10, 196.

Ronchetti, M. (2010). Using video lectures to make teaching more interactive. *International Journal of Emerging Technologies in Learning (iJET)* 5:2, 45–48.

Singhal, R., A. Singhal, M. Bhatnagar and N. Malhotra (2019). Design of an Audio Repository for Blind and Visually Impaired: A Case Study. In *Advanced Computing and Communication Technologies*. Singapore: Springer, 77–85.

Skylar, A. A. (2009). A Comparison of Asynchronous Online Text-based Lectures and Synchronous Interactive Web Conferencing Lectures. *Issues in Teacher education* 18:2, 69–84.

Van Zyl, H. and A. Powell Jr. (2012). Thomas Edison State College and Colorado State University: Using Cutting-edge Technology to Enhance CE Unit Success. *Continuing Higher Education Review* 76, 201–7.

Visser, J. A. (2000). Faculty Work in Developing and Teaching Web-based Distance Courses: A Case Study of Time and Effort. *American Journal of Distance Education* 14:3, 21–32.

6 Informal online resources and MOOCs

Nicky Nielsen

Perhaps the most explosive and rapid development of distance learning during the early years of the 21st century has been the Massive Open Online Courses (MOOCs). As interconnectivity improved and traditional (paid) online courses became more increasingly popular, MOOCs developed from the open educational resources (OER) movement, one which shares a great deal with the "open source" movement (to the extent that both can be grouped together as "open content"). At its core, a MOOC is a freely available online course which can recruit students numbering in the tens and even hundreds of thousands. While thousands of MOOCs are available through private suppliers such as Canvas Network, Udemy or Coursera, most still follow two basic pedagogical models, defined as xMOOCs or cMOOCs. xMOOCs tend to favour a more traditional teaching style, familiar from most distance education, one which seeks to a certain extent to emulate a physical classroom experience. Teaching is conducted via pre-recorded lectures, podcasts and discussion boards following a behaviourism learning theory. cMOOCs by contrast utilise connectivism and favour a far more student-led style of knowledge transfer utilising blog posts and social media, considering the students both learners and teachers.

Today, more than 100 million people worldwide have at some point signed up to one or more MOOCs (statistics from *By the Numbers: MOOCS in 2018*, compiled by Class Central). Large private providers, the biggest of which remains Coursera, have become major businesses, despite usually charging only very limited sums for their MOOCs by the standards of higher education in general (certainly in the United States and United Kingdom). Other providers, such as Canvas Network, have kept most of their courses free, although a plethora of different pricing systems are in play across the industry, from individual course subscription to a membership system to individual payments for certificates of completion or other micro-credentials at the end of the course. Most MOOCs are provided by educational establishments, with nearly a thousand universities worldwide having contributed one or more courses across the different platforms. A relatively recent development is the addition of MOOC degrees, starting with the University of the People in 2014 and Deakin University in Australia, which announced their suite of online degrees taught as MOOCs through FutureLearn in 2016. With less than 50 degree courses offered via MOOCs worldwide in 2019 and the number of new MOOC users falling from 2017 to 2018 by over 3 million, it is perhaps not yet clear to which extent the MOOC degrees will be a viable long-term solution. But they have underlined that MOOCs still have the potential to challenge perceptions about academia and the attainment of credentials.

As with all new teaching strategies and indeed most new technological developments, the appearance of MOOCs was received with a certain amount of scepticism from certain quarters and downright fear from others. In 2014, *The Guardian* newspaper asked its readers whether employers would ever take seriously a degree based even in part on MOOCs (*The Guardian*, June 12th 2014, "Will a degree made up of Moocs ever be worth the paper it's written on?"). Also writing in 2014, Ayala, Dick and Treadway conveyed a warning to university administrators and educators to take the development of MOOCs seriously and to engage with the new technology and method in a proactive manner rather than expecting the technology to simply "go away": "As such, one can view MOOCs as a threat, particularly to tier 2 and 3 schools – a 'disruptive technology' in information systems parlance. Industry is littered with failed businesses due to an inability to cope with a disruptive technology" (Ayala, Dick and Treadway 2014). Given the proliferation of MOOCs being produced by institutions of higher learning, it is clear that this warning was heeded to a certain extent.

A fundamental issue surrounding MOOCs, and perhaps the most virulent criticism of them, is the lack of quality control and the difficulty in accrediting them due to a lack of formal assessments (see for instance Gaebel 2014; Yuan and Powell 2013). Another point of criticism is the extent to which some providers have moved against the original concept of MOOCs as direct challengers to the high cost of formal education, spearheading a democratisation and spread of education worldwide:

> Massive Open Online Courses (MOOCs) would make courses from Harvard and MIT available free to anyone with an internet connection. The world's poor would finally have access to the same education as American ivy league students, while traditional fee paying higher education would go the way of relics like CDs and sailing ships.
>
> (Lodge 2013)

Lodge, writing in 2013, uses Udacity and its CEA Sebastian Thrun's decision to start charging for courses as an example of this, but there are several others. Writing in 2015, Michael Shea pointed out both the extreme naivety of universities in providing their content for free to for-profit companies such as Coursera but also criticised the lack of academic rigour and the meaningless certificates given to students upon completion (*The Skinny*, September 25th 2015, "MOOC: A University Qualification in 24 Hours?"). In addition, as raised by Adam (2019), most MOOCs are taught from Western universities and often marginalise and erode indigenous knowledge, creating a kind of "digital colonialism".

However, perhaps the most significant issue which continue to plague MOOC development is student retention. Multiple authorities have written on this topic (see in particular Paton, Fluck and Scanlan 2018). With some estimating average drop-out rates for MOOCs at 90% and above (Henderikx, Karel and Kalz 2017), a slew of papers have in recent years suggested various methodologies for predicting student behaviour, identifying students at risk of dropping out and adapting course structures to incentivise completion, for instance through assessment design (Olivé et al. 2019).

Given the experience and focus on distance learning Egyptology developed at the University of Manchester from the early 2000s onwards, it is unsurprising that MOOCs, mini-MOOCs and non-accredited Short Courses were relatively early on adapted as part of the broader suite of online courses. One major MOOC was launched on Coursera in 2015, Ancient Egypt in Six Objects, with a mini-MOOC, Warfare and Weapons in Ancient Egypt, hosted on Canvas following in 2017. In 2017 Ancient Egypt in Six Objects was moved from a tutor-led system on Coursera to an automatic system with self-marking assessments and no tutor support on Udemy. Upon its launch, Ancient Egypt in Six Objects attracted roughly 19,263 students worldwide, with a completion rate of 7%, broadly in line with general trends. Warfare and Weapons in Ancient Egypt attracted 856 students with a similar completion rate. Students were assessed via multiple choice questionnaires across the four-week course.

The aim behind the launch of these two MOOCs was twofold: (1) increase awareness of the Egyptology provision at Manchester and increase student recruitment numbers and (2) through cooperation with the Egyptology collection of Manchester Museum on the Six Objects MOOC, increase international awareness of the museum and its collection. In these goals, the MOOCs were both surprisingly successful. A significant uptick in the number of students applying for the more formal distance learning Egyptology courses with a nearly 40% increase in student intake on the Certificate in Egyptology followed the first running of Ancient Egypt in Six Objects, and a second increase following the running of Warfare and Weapons in Ancient Egypt.

Alongside these MOOCs, the DL provision at Manchester also includes several Short Courses (or online CPD Courses). These non-accredited units function as taster courses. They require no specific background knowledge or credentials, and the assessments are entirely formative, built around participation on relevant Blackboard discussion boards. The teaching is a mixture of written content, recorded lectures and podcasts. In terms of theme, the Short Course range from three levels of introductory Middle Egyptian Hieroglyphs and more historical topics such as Ancient Egyptian Gods and Goddesses. As with the MOOC provision, the Short Courses often function as a recruitment tool for the more formal accredited Egyptology courses, with prospective students utilising the Short Courses to gauge whether they can adjust and adapt to distance learning, in particular those with no prior DL experiences. This association is so clear that on several occasions drops in the student recruitment on Short Courses have a direct correlative effect on recruitment numbers on the three-year Certificate in Egyptology.

The key for any educator when proposing to launch a new course – whether that be a MOOC, a Short Course or a more formal offering – is to identify target audience and to answer the question: "What is the purpose of this course?" Given the free nature of many MOOCs, it is vital to identify the potential benefits in terms of recruitment numbers either directly feeding from the MOOC to the more formal course offering or alternatively through greater public awareness of a specific discipline or institution. This is by no means a call to consider all MOOCs as nothing more than glorified university pamphlets; a poorly presented MOOC with low student satisfaction and a high (or even higher than normal) drop-out rate will of course reflect poorly on the organising institution. And given the sheer reach of some MOOCs, bringing together hundreds of thousands of students throughout the world, such reputational damage can be severe and widespread.

MOOCs may not outcompete and take over typical face-to-face or even DL programmes within higher education as was predicted (and feared) in some quarters. But their reach is undeniable. They represent a way for institutions of higher learning not just to represent themselves to a broad and diverse audience but also to reach out to non-traditional students. When running the Warfare and Weapons in Ancient Egypt MOOC, I received an email from one of the students based in the United States. The student apologised for falling behind somewhat on completing the weekly multiple-choice quizzes and assured me that they would be catching up in the near future. The reason they provided was that they were currently homeless and participating in the course through the public library. The library they had customarily been using had closed and they had been forced to find another library some distance away. The student completed the course, despite their personal circumstances. MOOCs may at times come across as "faddish" or gimmicky. But their reach and the potential for student diversity is undeniable.

Works cited

Adam, T. (2019). Digital Neocolonialism and Massive Open Online Courses (MOOCs): Colonial Pasts and Neoliberal Futures. *Learning, Media and Technology* 44:3, 365–80.

Ayala, C., G. Dick and J. Treadway (2014). The MOOCs Are Coming! Revolution or Fad in the Business School? *Communications of the Association for Information Systems* 35, 226–44.

Gaebel, M. (2014). *MOOCs Massive Open Online Courses-an Update of EUA's First Paper (January 2013)*. EUA Occasional Papers: European University Association.

Henderikx, M. A., K. Karel and M. Kalz. (2017). Refining Success and Dropout in Massive Open Online Courses Based on the Intention–behavior Gap. *Distance Education* 38:3, 353–68.

Lodge, J. M. 2013. The Failure of Udacity: Lessons on Quality for Future MOOCs. *The Conversation*, November 19th 2013. Available from: https://theconversation.com/the-failure-of-udacity-lessons-on-quality-for-future-moocs-20416

Olivé, D. M., D. Q. Huynh, M. Reynolds, M. Dougiamas and D. Wiese. (2019). A Supervised Learning Framework: Using Assessment to Identify Students at Risk of Dropping Out of a MOOC. *Journal of Computing in Higher Education*, 1–18.

Paton, R. M., A. E. Fluck and J. D. Scanlan (2018). Engagement and Retention in VET MOOCs and Online Courses: A Systematic Review of Literature from 2013 to 2017. *Computers & Education* 125, 191–201.

Shea, M. (2015). MOOC: A University Qualification in 24 Hours or Less. *The Skinny*, September 25th. Available from: www.theskinny.co.uk/tech/features/moocs

Yuan, L. and S. Powell (2013). MOOCs and Disruptive Innovation: Implications for Higher Education. *eLearning Papers* 33. Available from: www.openeducationeuropa.eu/en/article/MOOCs-and-disruptive-innovation%3A-Implications-for-higher-education

7 Mumford the Mummy
Online Egyptology for children
Joyce Tyldesley

As technology and connectivity become more widely available, schools are increasingly employing digital tools and online learning resources to enhance traditional teacher-led lessons (Thibault et al. 2014: 458). Effectively, the classroom has become a blended space for both face-to-face and online learning. It therefore seems appropriate to end this book with a short but interesting case study detailing the creation of an online learning resource primarily aimed at English primary school pupils and their teachers.

The demands of the national curriculum

The "national curriculum" is a set of subjects and standards devised by the government to ensure that children in primary and secondary schools in England and Wales learn the same things. History is a compulsory national curriculum subject in primary schools. At Key Stage 2 (pupils aged 7–11), pupils in English schools are required to study, amongst other topics, "the achievements of the earliest civilizations – an overview of where and when the first civilizations appeared and an in-depth study of one of the following: Ancient Sumer; The Indus Valley; Ancient Egypt; The Shang Dynasty of Ancient China". Their teachers are required to "combine overview and depth studies to help pupils understand both the long arc of development and the complexity of specific aspects of the [syllabus] content." Even at primary school level, this is an onerous requirement for teachers who may have little or no knowledge of ancient Egypt.

Working with Mumford the Mummy

To help these teachers, Egyptology Online devised a thematic suite of digital learning resources based on a cartoon character. This was primarily an outreach project inspired by a wish to pay something back into the community, but it was also hoped that the challenge of working with a new platform and a new audience would have a positive effect on the university's more official online courses. *Ancient Egypt with Mumford the Mummy* emerged as a series of short, fun and innovative digital lessons covering

- geography and timeline,
- gods and goddesses,
- kings and queens,
- mummification and
- hieroglyphs.

Individual children, or children and their parents, can work with Mumford at home, but the target audience was primary school teachers who would use the learning resources in their classroom, moving from the traditional "sage on the stage" role to become the "guide on the side" (King 1993). The resources were therefore designed to engage a room full of pupils, with a mix of videos, jokes, interactive activities, quizzes, songs, creative writing and drawing activities. They utilise Nearpod software, making them accessible free of charge worldwide on any connected device.

Mumford and his friends were created by University of Manchester eLearning technologist Kate Hilton. Work commenced in October 2014, and the pilot resource was launched in January 2015. This was downloaded approximately 3,000 times in the first 12 weeks. The entire resource was re-launched for the 2015/16 academic year, and by mid-January 2016 had achieved 9,379 downloads, with the mummification lesson

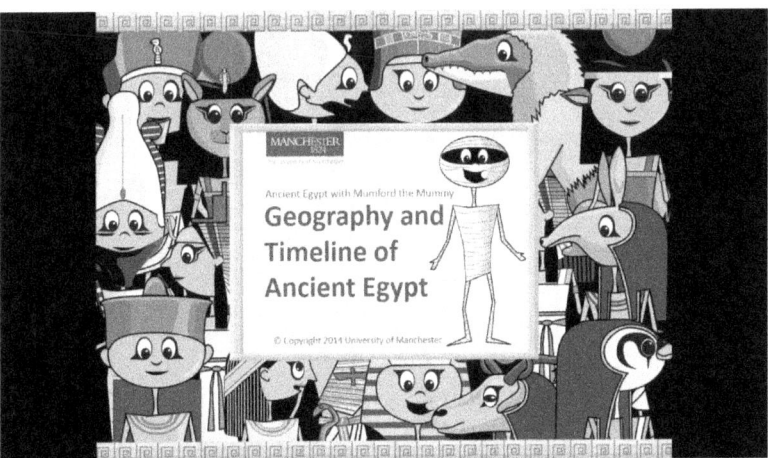

Figure 7.1 Mumford on Screen

proving the most popular. If we assume that each download is a teacher with a class of 25 children, the project had already had an outreach of over 300,000. Mumford continues to be available today: https://nearpod.com/s/universityofmanchester-A735944

Lessons learned from Mumford the Mummy

Many of the rules of creating an online resource apply equally to courses aimed at children and courses aimed at adults. All, for example, have to be accurate, engaging, stimulating and appropriate for level. However, there are additional aspects of working with children that needed to be considered when creating the Mumford learning resources.

From the outset, it was recognised that the material included in the lessons would have to be age appropriate. It was obvious that there should be no adult themes (no sex and violence, for example, and no bad language); this meant that thought had to be given to the presentation (or not) of subjects such as royal incest and the battles which occur from time to time in Egyptian history.

It was equally obvious that the children should not be subjected to potentially distressing images. Photographs of human remains and mummified animals and realistic drawings of human anatomy are likely to be considered unacceptable by some parents and teachers. The learning resource dealing with mummification was able to avoid any display of human remains

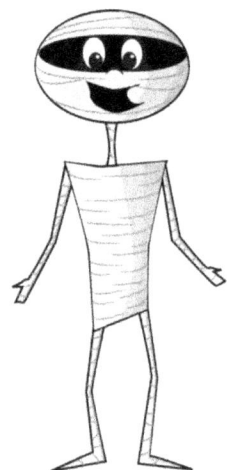

Figure 7.2 Mumford the Mummy

by showing the children how to mummify an orange, an easily repeatable classroom experiment that created an active learning environment.

Less immediately obvious were the potential problems surrounding the choice of a mummy as the children's friend and guide. The mummy is an instantly recognisable ancient Egyptian artefact, but it is also, of course, a dead Egyptian. Is it ever appropriate or respectful to use a dead character as entertainment? Does using a mummy send the wrong message about ancient Egypt, a society that was very much focused on the living rather than the dead? Eventually it was decided that Mumford's cheerful character and obviously artificial nature were sufficient to distance him from the realities of death and decay. The feedback received, although limited (there is no obvious means of collecting this feedback), has supported this decision: "My grandson age 10 is fascinated by Egypt and I think he'd love to interact with your adorable mummy" (feedback from 2017).

Works cited

Department for Education (2013). *History Programmes of Study: Key Stages 1 and 2 National Curriculum In England.* Reference: DFE-00173-2013.
King, A. (1993). From Sage on the Stage to Guide on the Side. *College Teaching* 41:1, 30–5.
Thibault, P., J. S. Curwood, L. Carvalho and A. Simpson (2014). Moving Across Physical and Online Spaces: A Case Study in a Blended Primary Classroom. *Learning, Media and Technology* 40:4, 458–79.

Conclusion
Helpful hints for setting up an online course

Joyce Tyldesley

I am concluding with a list of hints and suggestions based on the years of practical experience – some good, some less so – detailed in this book. I hope that you find it useful. Good luck with your own online course!

1. *Know your students.* How old are they? Where are they based? What other courses (if any) are they studying? What are their past learning experiences? Are they likely to be tech savvy or tech phobic? Your online course will need to be designed to suit your students' expectations and needs far more than a face-to-face course needs to be, so it makes sense to understand your audience as well as you can.
2. *Plan, plan and plan.* How are you going to present your work? Text? Lectures? Podcasts? A combination of all three and more? Will discussion boards be a key element of your teaching? You have the opportunity to be far more flexible than a face-to-face teacher bound by the tyranny of the timetable. So take some time to devise the teaching scheme that works best for you and your students.
3. *Err on the side of simplicity.* E-learning technologists are often keen to persuade online teachers to experiment with new (often untried) technologies. Resist this if you can. Unnecessary complexity can cause problems for staff and students who do not have a strong computer background and can prove impossible to operate for students lacking a good broadband connection. More importantly, technological complexity can obscure the core learning content. At Manchester, an experimental phase requiring students to write using a computer-generated hieroglyphic script soon degenerated into a computer course. Students became so fixated on mastering the computer programme, they started to ignore the hieroglyphs. Lesson learned: just because you can it doesn't mean that you should.
4. *Remember, consistency is key.* Create every work unit in the same style; use the same font and colour scheme; design icons and banners to

represent your course. A feeling of familiarity and belonging will prevent remote students from feeling lost when they log into their virtual classroom.
5 *Upload your course early.* It is entirely possible (though certainly not recommended) to pull a face-to-face lecture or seminar together an hour or so before it is delivered. If things go badly wrong, it is even possible to cancel a face-to-face teaching session. Online teachers do not have this option; they risk looking shamingly amateur if their course is not available at the stated time.
6 *Prepare in advance.* Online courses should ideally be prepared many weeks in advance. You know this; your institution may not. You may have planned to record lectures over the summer break, but the university may have planned to paint the lecture theatre that same week. They may not be prepared to work with you as far in advance as is necessary. Make your needs known.
7 *Upload your introduction last.* Although you have a tight syllabus for each work unit, record/write the introduction to your course last, as your plan will invariably vary slightly as you work your way through the course content.
8 *Do not be afraid to go back, but don't go back too often.* All teachers know what it feels like to give a bad lecture. In a face-to-face class this is an irretrievable situation; the lecture has been and gone. The online teacher has the option to rewrite or re-record; do not be afraid to do this where necessary. However, do not try to achieve perfection. Your students need to understand that they are not watching highly polished television documentaries: lecturers will cough, sneeze and stumble over words. That is an unavoidable part of real life, and they need to get used to it.
9 *Do not try to reinvent the wheel.* If there is an appropriate online resource available, don't be afraid to incorporate it into your course. Be aware, though, that you will have to check this imported material on a regular basis, as external resources are prone to disappear.
10 *Employ asynchronous teaching.* This is highly recommended as a means of allowing students to learn at a time and pace that suits them.
11 *Set a clear timetable.* Do not release all your learning material at once, as "self-paced" online learning can quickly grow out of control, making group teaching very difficult. Instead, roll out your learning modules gradually and set a clear cut-off date for each discussion board activity.
12 *Do not accidentally "date" your course.* No "good morning" or references to "today's news" or "earlier this week". Try also to avoid linking your lecture to another learning resource (so no "as we saw in the

previous lecture"), as this makes it less easy to reuse recorded material in a different context.
13. *Use guest lecturers.* Try to include guests in your teaching schedule. This can be difficult to organise in face-to-face teaching but relatively easy online. A new face, voice or approach will spark renewed student interest.
14. *Consider communication.* Will you accept student phone calls and emails about work (not recommended), or will you insist that all non-personal communication is processed through the teaching boards? How often will you be online? Will you have set "office hours"? How quickly will you respond to student posts? These decisions need to be made before the course is built, so that the students know from the outset how to communicate with you. Although the course is accessible 24/7, you do not have to be.
15. *Mind your netiquette.* Set very clear rules to ensure that the discussion boards are an accessible and safe space for both learners and teachers. These will include the obvious (no abuse or threatening behaviour) and the less obvious (no slang, no irony, no sarcasm). What sanctions will you impose if these rules are broken?
16. *Write a handbook.* Ensure that you have a well-written course handbook, which will enable your students to feel comfortable within their unfamiliar learning environment.
17. *Give appropriate information.* Your institution may have been very enthusiastic about introducing distance learning into the curriculum. But it may not have been entirely thought through. You may find that your students are unthinkingly being told that they must attend a welcome week, or hand in paper copies of their essays, or pop into the office to collect a student card. As far as you can, check that all peripheral material – departmental handbooks can be a problem here – is properly attuned to your students' requirements.
18. *Provide technical support.* Tell the students what is available and how it is to be accessed.
19. *Check your clocks.* It is important that students realise that you are working with UK (or your own local) time – they will need to calculate their own local equivalent to meet deadlines.
20. *Give visibility.* Show yourself to your students, introduce yourself, participate in icebreakers and give a personal response to all introductory posts: allow your students to feel a connection with you.
21. *Bond.* Allow your students to "meet" each other in an informal context (a virtual cafe or pub, perhaps) before formal teaching starts. This will lessen the feeling of isolation felt by some online learners.

22 *Remember that you will actually have to teach.* Simply putting material online and setting an assessed essay is not enough. Your students might as well read a book. Online teaching is increasingly becoming a necessity. It is also an art, a joy and a privilege. Don't be afraid to inject your own personality into your online teaching.

Index

Note: Italicized page numbers indicate a figure on the corresponding page.

3D environment 16–17

activity modules 46–9, *48*, 50–5
advance preparation considerations 87
age anxiety 38–9
Ancient Egyptian pedagogy online 21–3
Ancient Egypt with Mumford the Mummy course 82–5, *83*, *84*
anonymised discussion board 72
assessment strategies: cheating students 63–4; grading criteria responses 62–3; international students 62–3; introduction to 60–2; poor academic practices 63; quizzes 64; self-marking assessments 79; student feedback on 65
asynchronous teaching 87
attrition rates 23
audio-only lecture 71
augmented reality (AR) 16
Australian Council for Educational Research 8

Blackboard (virtual platform) 28–9, 61–2, 71, 73–4, 80
blended learning 2–3, 13, 43, 46, 73, 75, 82
blogs/blogging 3, 32, 77
bonding concerns 88
Boston Gazette 6, 11
broadband connections 40, 86

calendar tool 27
Canvas Network 77

Centre for Continuing Education 25, 26, 27
Certificate in Egyptology programme 3, 28–31, *30*
Certificate of Higher Education (CertHE) 26
Champollion, Jean-François 21–2
Chautauqua School of Languages 7
cheating students 63–4
child online Egyptology programmes 82–5, *83*, *84*
chronology development 24
Cleopatra VII, Queen 21
communication: email 47, 74; encouraging through community 50; expert-led 74; student-teacher 15, 88; technological development 67; tools to assist 11–12
community as online resource 55–7
compulsory activity modules 50–5
computer-based testing 60–1
computer skills 54
Continuing Education courses 24, 31
Correspondence Model 10–11
Coursera 77
credit-bearing programmes 55
criticism online 54
Crook and Flail, The (online community) 56
Cunningham, Kenneth 8

David, Rosalie 25, 27
Deakin University 78
digital camera 72

Index 91

Diploma Correspondence College 8
discussion boards: anonymised 72; community as online resource 55–7; student activities 41, 46–9, *48*
distance education: future of 16–18; historical methods 6–12; introduction to 6; origin of 6; present methods 12–15
Distributed Learning (DL) Unit 26
drop-out rates 13, 14
dynastic history 24

Edwards, Amelia B. 24
Edwards Professor of Egyptian Archaeology and Philology 24
Egyptology at University of Manchester: activity modules 46–9, *48*, 50–5; Ancient Egypt 21–3; in Britain 23–5; certificate programme 28–31, *30*; communication forms 15; community as online resource 55–7; e-lectures at 28, 69–73, *70*; face-to-face teaching 25–6, 27, 38, 40; faculty compliant programmes 27–8; introduction to 3, 21; MA in 34–7, *35*, *36*, *37*; netiquette 50; online courses 26–7, 32–4, *33*; overview of 25; postal teaching 25–6; Short Courses in Egyptology 31–2, 41; student feedback on 40–4, 57–9; student profile 37–40
e-learning: activities for 53; Egyptology at University of Manchester 28, 69–73, *70*; future of 16; introduction to 2; lectures and podcasts 66–9, 75; present methods 12–13; software development in 67
electronic detection system 64
email communication 47, 74
English-English spellings 62
essay-writing skills 61

Facebook 16, 32, 56
face-to-face teaching: commitments to studies 22; Egyptology at University of Manchester 25–6, 27, 38, 40; future of 18; introduction to 2–3; as key component 46; knowledge retention 67–8; mature versus younger students 51; present programmes 14; traditional night school courses 24–5
faculty compliant programmes 27–8
Faculty of Life Sciences (FLS) 27
feedback collection 40
Flexible Learning Model 11
flexible teaching 15, 16
flipped classroom approach 46–7
formally credited programmes 2
Foster, Thomas J. 9
Foulks Lynch Correspondence Tuition Service 8
French language learning 7
FutureLearn 78

Godenho, Glenn 28
Google Cardboard 16–18
grading criteria responses 62–3
group emails 74
Guardian, The (newspaper) 78
guest lecturers 88

Harper, William Rainey 7–8
Haworth, Jesse 25
Hebrew class 7
Hermod, Hans Svensson 9
Hermod Institute 9
hieroglyphic code: cracking of 22, 24; e-learning icons 29–30, *30*; tutors for 28
Hilton, Kate 83
Holmberg, B. 11
Hook, Sidney 2

individual activities 53
informal online resources 77–80
interactive multimedia (IMM) 11
International Correspondence School 9
international students 62–3
introversion in students 39
IT support team 1

job market concerns 24
Journal Club discussion board 41

KNH Centre for Biomedical Egyptology 27, 32
knowledge retention 67

Labels: A Mediterranean Journal (Waugh) 74

Labour Government (UK) 9–10
Langenscheidt, Gustav 7
lectures and podcasts: introduction to 66; overview of 66–9; student survey results 73–5; summary of 75; vlogs and 73–5
live lecture recordings 12
live-streaming 11, 68–9
Lunds Weckoblad (newspaper) 7

MA in Egyptology 34–7, *35*, *36*, *37*
Malmö Språk-och Handelsinstitut (Malmö Language and Mercantile Institute) 9
Massive Online Open Courses (MOOCs) 2–3, 24, 77–80
mature students 18, 38, 51
Mine Safety Act (1885) 8
Mining Herald, The (newspaper) 9
Multi-Media Model 11
multiple-choice quizzes 64
Mumford the Mummy programme 82–5, *83*, *84*
Mummy, The (film) 22
mummy studies 25
museum websites 3, 14, 23–4

national curriculum demands 82
Nearpod software 83
netiquette 50, 88
newsgroups 3
Nielsen, Nicky 28
non-accredited units 79–80
non-Egyptophiles 3
non-native English speakers 61
non-traditional students 18

Oculus Rift 16–17
Office for National Statistics 28
one-off substitutions 64
online Egyptology programmes: for children 82–5, *83*, *84*; Egyptology at University of Manchester 26–7, 32–4, *33*; helpful hints for 86–9; introduction to 1–4
open book essays 61
open educational resources (OER) movement 77
"open source" movement 77

Open University: history of 4n1, 10; introduction to 1; present usage 13; television medium in 66

Personal Portfolio 51, 55
Petrie, Flinders 24
Philipps, Caleb 6
Pitman, Isaac 7
plagiarism concerns 61, 64
podcasts *see* lectures and podcasts
postal teaching 25–6
PowerPoint 71, 72
prerecorded lectures 67–8
problem-based learning 39

quizzes as assessment strategies 64

radio station learning 9
retention by students 6–7, 14–15, 30, 67–8, 75, 79
risk landscape 39
Rosetta Stone 21–2
rota system 27
Ruskin College 7

satisfaction by students 11, 52, 68, 71, 75, 80
self-learning/teaching methods 7, 22
self-marking assessments 79
sense of belonging 47
Shea, Michael 78–9
Short Courses in Egyptology 31–2, 41, 71–2, 79–80
short credit-bearing courses 2
shorthand writing 7
Society to Encourage Studies at Home 7
software development 67
sound booth needs 71
spirituality of the past 22
staff-student liaisons 41
stationary digital camera 72
Stobart, J.C. 10
storytelling online 12
student cards 14
student profile in Egyptology at University of Manchester 37–40
Student Representatives 41
student retention 6–7, 14–15, 30, 67–8, 75, 79

Index

student satisfaction 11, 52, 68, 71, 75, 80
student–student contact 26
students with caring responsibilities 18
student-to-student mentoring 15
student–tutor contact 26
study-skills 26, 56, 61

Taylor, J.C. 10–11
teaching concerns 89
technical support 88
telecommunication technologies 12
Telelearning Model 11
televised universities 6
text-based learning modules 27
Theodosius, Emperor 21
Thrun, Sebastian 78–9
Ticknor, Anna Eliot 7
timelines 24
timetable setting 87
time zone considerations 68, 69
Toussaint, Charles 7
traditional teaching 15
tuition fees 2, 8, 47, 49
tutorial discussion groups 49
tutors/tutoring 60
tutor–tutor contact 26
tweets/tweeting 3
Tyldesley, Joyce 27–8
"Tyranny of Isolation" 10

Udacity 78–9
Udemy 77
UK-English spellings 62
University College London 24
University Correspondence College 8

university library online resources 61
University of London 7
University of Manchester *see* Egyptology at University of Manchester
University of Manchester Worldwide (UMW) 5n5
University of Melbourne 17
University of Queensland 8
University of the People 78
University of West Virginia 8
University of Wisconsin 8
uploading courses 87
US-English spellings 62

video capture system 71–2
video editing software 72
virtual classrooms *see* online Egyptology programmes
Virtual Learning Environment 26, 69
virtual reality (VR) 16–17
visibility concerns 89
vlog lectures 73–5

Waugh, Evelyn 74
WebCT platform 27, 28, 69, 71
Williams, R.C.G. 10
Wilson, Harold 9–10
Wimba 69
women's programmes 7
Worker's Education Association 24–5
World Wide Web (WWW) 10, 11
written coursework/materials 60, 66

younger students 2, 38–9, 51, 53

For Product Safety Concerns and Information please contact our EU representative GPSR@taylorandfrancis.com
Taylor & Francis Verlag GmbH, Kaufingerstraße 24, 80331 München, Germany

www.ingramcontent.com/pod-product-compliance
Lightning Source LLC
Chambersburg PA
CBHW070741230426
43669CB00014B/2531